HOPE

An Anchor for Life

DR. DAVID JEREMIAH

with Dr. David Jeremiah

CONTENTS

About Dr. David Jeremiah and Turning Point 4

How to Use This Study Guide 5

Introduction 11

1. Hope—An Anchor for Life
   Hebrews 6 13

2. Hope in God
   Psalms 42 and 43 29

3. A Living Hope
   1 Peter 1 45

4. Hope in the Valley of Trouble
   Joshua 7; Hosea 2:15 61

5. A Psalm of Hope
   Psalm 146 77

6. Hope for Our Nation
   2 Kings 22 and 23 91

7. Hope for Our Church
   Selected Scriptures 107

8. Hope for Our Families
   Selected Scriptures 125

Additional Resources 142

Stay Connected 144

ABOUT DR. DAVID JEREMIAH AND TURNING POINT

D r. David Jeremiah is the founder of Turning Point, a ministry committed to providing Christians with sound Bible teaching relevant to today's changing times through radio and television broadcasts, audio series, books, and live events. Dr. Jeremiah's common-sense teaching on topics such as family, prayer, worship, angels, and biblical prophecy forms the foundation of Turning Point.

David and his wife, Donna, reside in El Cajon, California, where he serves as the senior pastor of Shadow Mountain Community Church. David and Donna have four children and twelve grandchildren.

In 1982, Dr. Jeremiah brought the same solid teaching to San Diego television that he shares weekly with his congregation. Shortly thereafter, Turning Point expanded its ministry to radio. Dr. Jeremiah's inspiring messages can now be heard worldwide on radio, television, and the Internet.

Because Dr. Jeremiah desires to know his listening audience, he travels nationwide holding ministry rallies and spiritual enrichment conferences that touch the hearts and lives of many people. According to Dr. Jeremiah, "At some point in time, everyone reaches a turning point; and for every person, that moment is unique, an experience to hold onto forever. There's so much changing in today's world that sometimes it's difficult to choose the right path. Turning Point offers people an understanding of God's Word as well as the opportunity to make a difference in their lives."

Dr. Jeremiah has authored numerous books, including *Escape the Coming Night* (Revelation), *The Handwriting on the Wall* (Daniel), *Overcoming Loneliness, Prayer—The Great Adventure, God in You* (Holy Spirit), *When Your World Falls Apart, My Heart's Desire, 31 Days to Happiness—Searching for Heaven on Earth, Captured by Grace, Grace Givers, Signs of Life, What in the World Is Going On?, The Coming Economic Armageddon, I Never Thought I'd See the Day!, God Loves You: He Always Has—He Always Will, What Are You Afraid Of?, Agents of the Apocalypse,* and *RESET—Ten Steps to Spiritual Renewal.*

How to Use This Study Guide

The purpose of this Turning Point study guide is to reinforce Dr. David Jeremiah's dynamic, in-depth teaching and to aid the reader in applying biblical truth to his or her daily life. This study guide is designed to be used in conjunction with Dr. Jeremiah's *Hope—An Anchor for Life* audio series, but it may also be used by itself for personal or group study.

Structure of the Lessons

Each lesson is based on one of the messages in the *Hope—An Anchor for Life* compact disc series and focuses on specific passages in the Bible. Each lesson is composed of the following elements:

- *Outline*

The outline at the beginning of the lesson gives a clear, concise picture of the topic being studied and provides a helpful framework for readers as they listen to Dr. Jeremiah's teaching.

- *Overview*

The overview summarizes Dr. Jeremiah's teaching on the passage being studied in the lesson. Readers should refer to the Scripture passages in their own Bibles as they study the overview. Unless otherwise indicated, Scripture verses quoted are taken from the New King James Version.

- *Personal and Group Application Questions*

This section contains a variety of questions designed to help readers dig deeper into the lesson and the Scriptures, and to apply the lesson to their daily lives. For Bible study groups or Sunday school classes, these questions will provide a springboard for group discussion and interaction.

- *Did You Know?*

This section presents a fascinating fact, historical note, or insight that adds a point of interest to the preceding lesson.

PERSONAL STUDY

Thank you for selecting *Hope—An Anchor for Life* for your current study. The lessons in this study guide were created to help you gain fresh insights into God's Word and develop new perspectives on topics you may have previously studied. Each lesson is designed to challenge your thinking, and help you grow in your knowledge of Christ. During your study, it is our prayer that you will discover how biblical truth affects every aspect of your life and your relationship with Christ will be strengthened.

When you commit to completing this study guide, try to set apart a time, daily or weekly, to read through the lessons without distraction. Have your Bible nearby when you read the study guide, so you're ready to look up verses if you need to. If you want to use a notebook to write down your thoughts, be sure to have that handy as well. Take your time to think through and answer the questions. If you plan on reading the study guide with a small group, be sure to read ahead and be prepared to take part in the weekly discussions.

LEADER'S GUIDE

Thank you for your commitment to lead a group through *Hope—An Anchor for Life*. Being a leader has its own rewards. You may discover that your walk with the Lord deepens through this experience. Throughout the study guide, your group will explore new topics and review study questions that encourage thought-provoking group discussion.

The lessons in this study guide are suitable for Sunday school classes, small-group studies, elective Bible studies, or home Bible study groups. Each lesson is structured to provoke thought and help you grow in your knowledge and understanding of God. There are multiple components in this section that can help you structure your lessons and discussion time, so make sure you read and consider each one.

Before You Begin

Before you begin each meeting, make sure you and your group are well-versed with the content of the chapter. Every person should have his or her own study guide so they can follow along and write in the study guide if need be. When possible, the study guide should be used with the corresponding compact disc series. You may wish to assign the study guide lesson as homework prior to the meeting of the group and then use the meeting time to listen to the CD and discuss the lesson.

To ensure that everyone has a chance to participate in the discussion, the ideal size for a group is around 8-10 people. If there are more than 10 people, try to break up the bigger group into smaller subgroups. Make sure the members are committed to participating each week, as this will help create stability and help you better prepare the structure of the meeting.

At the beginning of the study each week, start the session with a question to challenge group members to think about the issues you will be discussing. The members can answer briefly, but the goal is to have an idea in their mind as you go over the lesson. This allows the group members to become engaged and ready to interact with the group.

After reviewing the lesson, try to initiate a free-flowing discussion. Invite group members to bring questions and insights they may have discovered to the next meeting, especially if they were unsure of the meaning of some parts of the lesson. Be prepared to discuss how biblical truth applies to the world we live in today.

Weekly Preparation

As the group leader, here are a few things you can do to prepare for each meeting:

- Choose whether or not you will play the CD message during your small group session.

  If you decide to play the CD message from Dr. Jeremiah as part of the meeting, you will need to adjust the group time accordingly.

- Make sure you are thoroughly familiar with the material in the lesson.

  Make sure you understand the content of the lesson so you know how to structure group time and you are prepared to lead group discussion.

- Decide, ahead of time, which questions you plan to discuss.

  Depending on how much time you have each week, you may not be able to reflect on every question. Select specific questions which you feel will evoke the best discussion.

- Take prayer requests.

  At the end of your discussion, take prayer requests from your group members and pray for each other.

Structuring the Discussion Time

If you need help in organizing your time when planning your group Bible study, here are two schedules, for sixty minutes and ninety minutes, which can give you a structure for the lesson:

Option 1 (Listen to Audio CD)	60 Minutes	90 Minutes
Welcome: Members arrive and get settled.	N/A	5 minutes
Getting Started Question: Prepares the group for interacting with one another.	Welcome and Getting Started 5 minutes	15 minutes
Message: Listen to the audio CD.	40 minutes	40 minutes
Discussion: Discuss group study questions.	10 minutes	25 minutes
Prayer and Application: Final application for the week and prayer before dismissal.	5 minutes	5 minutes

Option 2 (No Audio CD)	60 Minutes	90 Minutes
Welcome: Members arrive and get settled.	5 minutes	10 minutes
Getting Started Question: Prepares the group for interacting with one another.	10 minutes	10 minutes
Message: Review the lesson.	15 minutes	25 minutes
Discussion: Discuss group study questions.	25 minutes	35 minutes
Prayer and Application: Final application for the week and prayer before dismissal.	5 minutes	10 minutes

As the group leader, it is up to you to keep track of the time and keep things moving along according to your schedule. If your group is having a good discussion, don't feel the need to stop and move on to the next question. Remember, the purpose is to pull together ideas, and share unique insights on the lesson. Make time each week to discuss how to apply these truths to living for Christ today.

The purpose of discussion is for everyone to participate, but don't be concerned if certain group members are more quiet—they may be internally reflecting on the questions and need time to process their ideas before they can share them.

Group Dynamics

Leading a group study can be a rewarding experience for you and your group members—but that doesn't mean there won't be challenges. Certain members may feel uncomfortable discussing topics that they consider very personal, and might be afraid of being called on. Some members might have disagreements on specific issues. To help prevent these scenarios, consider the following ground rules:

- If someone has a question that may seem off topic, suggest that it is discussed at another time, or ask the group if they are okay with addressing that topic.

- If someone asks a question you don't know the answer to, confess that you don't know and move on. If you feel comfortable, invite other group members to give their opinions, or share their comments based on personal experience.

- If you feel like a couple of people are talking much more than others, direct questions to people who may not have shared yet. You could even ask the more dominating members to help draw out the quiet ones.

- When there is a disagreement, encourage the group members to process the matter in love. Invite members from opposing sides to evaluate their opinions and consider the ideas of the other members. Lead the group through Scripture that addresses the topic, and look for common ground.

When issues arise, remind your group to think of Scripture: "Love one another" (John 13:34), "If it is possible, as much as depends on you, live peaceably with all men" (Romans 12:18), and "Be quick to listen, slow to speak and slow to become angry" (James 1:19, NIV).

FOR CONTINUING STUDY

For a complete listing of Dr. Jeremiah's materials for personal and group study call 1-800-947-1993, go online to www.DavidJeremiah.org, or write to Turning Point, P.O. Box 3838, San Diego, CA 92163.

Dr. Jeremiah's *Turning Point* program is currently heard or viewed around the world on radio, television, and the Internet in English. *Momento Decisivo*, the Spanish translation of Dr. Jeremiah's messages, can be heard on radio in every Spanish speaking country in the world. The television broadcast is also broadcast by satellite throughout the Middle East with Arabic subtitles.

Contact Turning Point for radio and television program times and stations in your area, or visit our website at www.DavidJeremiah.org/stationlocator.

HOPE—AN ANCHOR FOR LIFE

INTRODUCTION

How many times do we say the word *hope* without even considering what it truly means? For some, hope can mean a wish, a goal, a dream, or even a longing. Too often we state we *hope* to do something or go somewhere, when what we really mean is that we *wish* or *want* to do something. There is something so inspiring when you see people who are in a position where they could lose hope, but instead they put their confidence in God. The flooding in southern Louisiana in 2016 was a tremendous example. Without warning, heavy rains caused unprecedented flooding of towns and neighborhoods—causing hundreds of people's homes and possessions, as well as businesses, to be lost in a span of 24 hours. But even as families returned home to ruined homes, many thanked God for the safety of their loved ones and reached out to their neighbors to help them as well. If their job was still there, they went to work and began what was next in rebuilding their lives. While no one dismissed how difficult and challenging this task was going to be, their hope was not in the things they had lost, but in their hope for the future.

These people displayed a deep-seated hope for the future that was not caught up in worldly possessions—even as necessary as they are for our comfort. Many people today do not have that kind of hope—their confidence is firmly placed in things that are temporal, and while they may be important in the moment, once the object of hope is gone, people often become depressed and experience hopelessness. The loss could be a job, a relationship, a scholarship, a game, or even a home. True hope is a faith-based confidence and expectation in the only One who will never let us down.

Sadly, we live in a day when many of people have lost hope. According to Healthline Networks, "44 percent of American college students report having symptoms of depression." One student from the University of Michigan, a twenty-year-old junior said, "I was just completely unmotivated to do anything other than pretty much just sit in my room and lie there and look at the wall—that was about it." Only with counseling and medication was she able to regain a hopeful perspective on her future.

Why are people losing hope? Given the state of the world we live in, it's easy to understand how it happens. If one's only source of hope is found in the things of this world, that represents a tenuous source of hope at best. Wars, terrorist attacks, incurable diseases, poverty, natural disasters—how hopeful are these events? Fortunately, the Bible says that the things of this world are passing away (1 John 2:17). Unfortunately, for the person who has hoped only in the things of this world, it means all their sources of hope are passing away. What's a hopeless person to do?

Hope—An Anchor for Life has been prepared to restore hope to the hopeless. Many in our world do not know it, but the Bible presents a lifetime of reasons to have hope! Besides the hope of eternal life in heaven that is promised to all who belong to Jesus Christ (John 3:16), there is reason to have hope regardless of daily circumstances. The eight lessons in this study guide, along with the personal and group application questions for further study following each chapter, will provide a biblical framework for hope—today, tomorrow, and for all eternity.

HOPE—AN ANCHOR FOR LIFE

Hebrews 6

*In this lesson we are introduced to the hope
we have in Christ.*

OUTLINE

If you have ever seen an aircraft carrier or a cruise ship tied to a dock, you know what must be required to keep those boats in place. But it takes an even stronger anchor to keep the human soul in place in the face of life's challenges. Hope, rooted in Christ, is the anchor of our soul.

I. **The Necessity of Hope**
   A. Hope Is Necessary Because Often the Way Is Unknown
   B. Hope Is Necessary Because Often the Waiting Is Uncontrollable
   C. Hope Is Necessary Because Often the Will Is Uncooperative
   D. Hope Is Necessary Because Often the Waters Are "Unchartable"

II. **The Qualities of Hope**
   A. Hope Is Sure
   B. Hope Is Steadfast
   C. Hope Is Secure

OVERVIEW

In this first lesson, I want to begin by reminding you of something you have most likely observed; one of the most overwhelming emotions of our time is despair. Along with despair, hopelessness and helplessness have become buzzwords in many of the conversations that we have from day to day.

More and more, people feel as if nothing they can do is going to make a difference in the world. Although I don't have all the answers to this issue, one thing I know for certain is you can't live very long without hope. Hope is the very stuff of life. It's at the very core of who you are as a person.

I have a fascinating book in my library called *Learned Optimism*, written by a sociologist from the University of Pennsylvania by the name of Martin Seligman. Among his many excellent points, he concludes that hopelessness and helplessness are not natural responses we are born with, rather they are learned responses. No one is born hopeless. Children may be born into families where hope is modeled and cultivated, but that hope can be dashed as the child grows and experiences disappointments through people and events in their lives.

Seligman made an observation in his book to illustrate his point about hopelessness and helplessness: Children do get depressed—but there is a striking difference with children. Children below the age of seven never commit suicide. Above age seven, especially among teenagers, there are tens of thousands of suicides each year. Suicide among young people almost always follows a bout of depression and hopelessness. In fact, the combination of depression and hopelessness is the most accurate predictor of suicide.

Those who have lost hope believe that their condition is going to last forever, so they choose to end their life rather than suffer forever. In contrast, young children do not view discouragement or hopelessness as final. They are filled with hope and can bounce back from difficult circumstances.[1]

We all love the sense of optimism and innocence that children possess, don't we? A child can stand at the foot of an escalator and believe it reaches all the way to God. However, it doesn't remain without effort. And that is Seligman's point. We learn to be hopeless. We learn to feel helpless. We either learn to be hopeless or hopeful, or learn to be helpless or helpful.

Life has a way of setting us on a tough course if we do not have something at the center of our lives holding us steady.

Another book I read years ago, written by a famous magazine editor by the name of Norman Cousins, is called *Anatomy of an Illness*. He tells his own story of being diagnosed with a life-threatening disease, and his doctors told him he would not be able to recover. He rejected their verdict of certain death and decided that if he was going to die, he would die laughing. As an experiment, he combined taking large doses of vitamins and laughing. He collected Laurel and Hardy movies, old comedy routines, and joke books. He spent eight to ten hours every day watching funny movies and laughing—and he got better!

Ultimately, his disease went away, and he was asked to join the faculty of the University of Southern California medical school to explore the impact of hope and optimism on disease. For ten years, he researched the concept of hope in terms of healing, and came away with enough material to write a book called *Head First: The Biology of Hope*. In it, he assessed the impact of hope on sick people, and his studies showed a high correlation between those with hope and those who conquered their disease.

Of that experiment and discovery, Cousins later wrote:

People tell me not to offer hope unless I know hope to be real, but I don't have the power not to respond to an outstretched hand. I don't know enough to say that hope can't be real. I'm not sure anybody knows enough to deny hope. I've seen too many cases these past 10 years when death predictions were delivered from high professional stations only to be gloriously refuted by patients for reasons having to do less with tangible biology than with the human spirit. The human spirit may be admittedly a vague term, but it is probably the greatest force within the human arsenal for dealing with discouragement and disease.[2]

If you remember anything from these quotations of Norman Cousins, remember this final statement: "Don't deny the diagnosis, but defy the verdict."[3]

How many of us in our lives have faced challenges? Everybody around us is going to tell us how bad it's going to be and why it won't work out and how we can't do it. We cannot deny the diagnosis, but by the faith that is in us through Jesus Christ, we can defy the verdict! With God there is always hope!

In this study guide we are going to examine the life-sustaining reality of hope based on the foundational principles of Scripture. It is through a study of the Word of God throughout one's life that hope is cultivated (learned) and maintained. At the end of this study,

Hope Is Steadfast

Second, hope is steadfast, which means it is not going to change. It will keep our soul from moving regardless of the forces that try to move it off the path of our journey.

Hope Is Secure

Third, hope is secure, for it has entered in behind the veil and it is fastened there.

When God gave Abraham the promise that he was going to have a son and he would be the father of a new nation, there were two undeniable proofs of that promise: First, He gave him a promise. Second, He gave him an oath. In the promise, God cannot lie (He is sure). In the oath, God cannot change (He is steadfast).

The third characteristic—secure—is bound in the imagery of nautical experiences the writer of Hebrews used. In the days of Paul and the New Testament writers, there was a procedure used to bring large ships into harbors and ports. They had a rock that was embedded into the granite dock in the harbor. Literally, the rock was called the anchorea, the word from which we get our word "anchor." When a larger ship would come into the harbor they would disembark two or three of their chief hands into small boats, and they would take the anchor rope with them and fasten it to the rock embedded in the granite. And the boat trying to safely get into the harbor would follow the strength of that rope.

That is the image the writer uses in verse 19 with reference to Christ. He tells us Jesus Christ is our forerunner and He has carried our anchor behind the veil into the very presence of God. He has affixed our hope there so we can move through life into turbulent waters and troubled times and still have a secure anchor. Our anchor is Christ and we follow Him. Boat anchors may go down downward in the sea but ours goes upward toward heaven!

The great writer A. W. Tozer put it this way: "The man who comes to a right belief about God is relieved of ten thousand temporal problems, for he sees at once that these problems do not have to do with matters which at the most cannot concern him for very long."[4] This means that whenever problems come that might destroy our hope—even ten thousand of them—we are not shaken because our anchor is Jesus Christ who is in the very presence of God.

I've always been a fan of mystery stories, and there was never a better teller of those tales than Alfred Hitchcock. His episodes have been off prime time T.V. for quite a few years, but they were gripping tales when they were played out. One of his stories involved a rather wicked, two-faced woman who murdered a person and was sentenced to life in prison. On the day of her sentencing, she erupted angrily at the judge, screaming that she didn't care where he sent her, that she would escape one day and come back to haunt him.

On the day she was taken to the prison, she noticed an old man, an inmate, covering up a grave in a small cemetery outside the prison walls. He not only buried the inmates who died in the prison, he also built their caskets and rolled them outside on a cart to the cemetery. She realized that with his access to the gate, she needed to convince him to help her escape.

When she met the old man, she realized that he was going blind with cataracts on his eyes; and she took that as her means of enticing him into her plan. She told him if he would help her escape, she had enough money on the outside to pay for his going to a doctor to have cataracts removed from his eyes. At first the old man refused to help her. But she worked on him every day, reminding him that she was his only chance to have the operation he needed, and he finally gave in.

They devised a plan. The next time she heard the tolling of the prison bell that signaled a death in the prison, she would slip down to the shop where he built the caskets and get in the casket with the deceased inmate and pull the top down tightly. The next morning the old man would roll the casket, with her in it, to the cemetery where he would put the casket in the grave and cover it with dirt. The next day he was to come back, scrape away the dirt, release the top on the casket, and set the woman free.

A perfect plan—almost. The next time she heard the bell toll late at night, she made her way to the old man's dark shop, found the casket and removed the lid, lay down next to the corpse, and replaced the lid. The next morning, she could feel the casket being moved and rolled outside the gates to the cemetery. She smiled as the casket was lowered into the hole, and the clods of dirt began to fall on the lid. Her plan had worked to perfection, or so she thought.

The next day, no one came to free her. She waited what seemed to be hours and was growing worried and frightened. She had been buried alive, and there was no one to set her free. She couldn't imagine what had gone wrong with her plan.

In a state of panic, she struck a match to look around and glanced at the corpse next to her, only to see that it was the old man himself who had died the night before! She had been buried with the one who was to be her salvation. Her hopes for freedom were buried with her in her grave, never to be fulfilled or experienced.

That's a macabre tale to tell to illustrate a spiritual point, but perhaps its shock value will cause us to remember its application forever: Many people's hopes are buried with them in the grave. They live their whole lives never experiencing the fulfillment of their spiritual hopes, never coming to know the hope of eternal life in Christ. As Paul wrote in 1 Corinthians 15, "If in this life only we have hope in Christ, we are of all men the most pitiable" (verse 19).

We would be the most pitiable of all people if we did not have an anchor that goes beyond the veil in the presence of God. If we don't have hope in Someone who is going to survive all of the challenges we face, then we have no hope.

I want to tell you about Someone who went into the grave, Someone who didn't need anybody to come and get Him out. Of His own power, He came victoriously out of that tomb and raised His fist up as if to say, "If you believe in Me, you shall live also!" When you put your trust in Christ, you have the hope of the resurrection. He is the anchor to which our rope is tied, the anchor that gives us hope that we will one day be where He is.

As we begin this series of eight lessons on the biblical doctrine of hope, I have to begin by asking you whether your hope is in Jesus Christ. If you have never put your faith in Him as a deliberate choice and act, now would be a perfect time to do so. Just tell God that you want Christ to be your hope, and you will have it—a hope sufficient to take you through time into eternity.

Notes:

1. Martin E. P. Seligman, *Learned Optimism* (New York: A. A. Knopf, 1991), 126.
2. Quoted in Jesse A. Stoff, M.D., *The Prostrate Miracle* (New York: Kensington Publishing Corp, 2000), 188.
3. Norman Cousins, quoted in Abe Arkoff, *Psychology and Personal Growth* (Boston: Allyn & Bacon, 1988), 298.
4. A. W. Tozer, *The Knowledge of the Holy* (San Francisco: Harper & Row, 1978), 2.

1. Read Hebrews 6:13-20.

    a. When God made a promise to Abraham, how did Abraham know that he could trust God? (verse 13) How does this encourage you to trust God?

    b. How did Abraham respond to the promise, before obtaining it? (verse 15) What response do you usually have while waiting on the Lord?

c. According to verse 18, what reason do you have to trust in God and have hope in His promises?

d. What are the qualities of hope according to verses 19-20? In what situations do you find it difficult to put your trust in the Living Hope? Why?

e. Who has become our secure access into the Presence behind the veil? (verse 20) List all the worries you have been struggling with and have yet to give to Christ.

f. How can Psalm 46:10 reassure you to let go of these worries?

2. According to Ephesians 2:12, what is it like to be without God? Can you remember a time in your life when you've felt overwhelmingly hopeless? How can verse 13 provide inspiration for you, when you feel alone?

1. Read Hebrews 10:19-25.

   a. What exhortation do you find concerning hope in verse 23a?

   b. Discuss the importance of this idea in the Christian life. What might happen if Christians don't do this?

   c. What reason is given in verse 23b for not "wavering" with regard to hope? Talk about steps you can take to grow your trust in God. Give examples of ways you can learn to put your trust in Him.

d. What is the basis of our "full assurance of faith"? (verses 19-21)

e. How is "hope" different from "hope based on Jesus"? In what
   sense is the object of hope just as important as the object of
   one's faith? Share with the group a time when the Lord came
   through for you in a time of hopelessness.

f. How important is "consider[ing] one another" (verse 24) to keeping hope alive? How easy is it to become hopeless when you are alone? How do verses 24-25 apply to your study group?

g. What kinds of encouragement would be helpful for a person whose hope was wavering? (verse 25) Discuss how you can encourage people around you who seem like they need it.

h. Share a time when fellow believers in your life encouraged you when your hope and faith were wavering. What did they do or say? How did they exhort you?

i. How can your group learn from that example?

j. Discuss current situations where it is easy to lose hope. What have you learned from this passage in Hebrews that you can apply to your life?

DID YOU KNOW?

There is one place in Scripture where followers of Christ are told not to have hope. The noun for hope is Greek *elpis* while the verb, to have hope, is *elpizo*. The negative form of *elpizo* is *apelpizo* in the New Testament is in Luke 6:35 where Christ says to "love your enemies, do good, and lend, hoping for nothing (*apelpizo*) in return." Therefore, when it comes to doing good, we are to do it without hope of return in this life (though there is hope of reward in heaven).

HOPE IN GOD

Psalms 42 and 43

In this lesson we explore three paradoxes about how hope rises in the heart.

OUTLINE

When we are in a discouraging place, the last thing we anticipate experiencing is hope. But that is the very thing we should expect! We don't need hope when things are going well. We need hope when all hope has been lost. It is when we least expect hope that it will most likely appear.

I.   **Hope Is Most Alive When Everything Seems Hopeless**

II. **Hope for the Future Is Built on the Past**

III. **Hope Sings When It Feels Like Crying**

OVERVIEW

A Jewish friend of mine had a successful business that he had built from scratch. He had always dreamed of someday turning it over to his son. He prided himself in the fact that this was one of those classic father-son enterprises that could only get better with time.

His son was any father's dream. He was athletic, handsome, and had a charismatic personality. Unfortunately, he was also very wild. On more than one occasion, my friend shook his head and wondered if his boy would ever be mature enough to take over the business when his time came.

One day, however, he learned that his son had no intention of waiting until it was his turn to run the company. This enterprising rebel went to all the employees and, one by one, persuaded them to believe that they would be much better off if he (the son) was running things instead of his father. Over time he infiltrated the board of directors, and they eventually voted to remove the father from his position as Chairman and CEO, and they put the son in his place.

The son had plotted a takeover and succeeded. The father was left to clean out his office. There was nothing he could do. He couldn't even go back into the building. He rented some office space across the street, and he sat there by the hour looking out the window at what was once his, mourning the betrayal of his own flesh and blood, feeling about as hopeless and helpless as any man could feel.

My Jewish friend's name was David. And his son's name was Absalom. I changed a few of the details to hide their identities, but the basic plot is the same. Absalom sat by the gate of the city, and everyone who came in and out of the city where his father was king were told they would be much better off if they had a more accessible leader. He persuaded many of the people and leaders to turn against his father.

David ultimately had to leave the city with a few of his close friends. The geographical details given to us in Psalm 42 tell us that his location was across the Jordan River on the other side of the valley. There, he mourned the loss of his kingdom, the betrayal of his son, and the feeling of being abandoned by God. Shut out from God's presence, shut out from worship in the temple, and shut out by his own son. Psalms 42-43 give us the details of what he thought and felt.

The fact that these two psalms go together is supported by one thought that occurs three times: "Why are you cast down, O my soul? And why are you disquieted within me? Hope in God . . ." (42:5, 11; 43:5). The inscription over Psalm 42 was addressed to the choir master and it is called a Maskil of the sons of Korah. The word *maskil* in Hebrew means it is a teaching Psalm. Therefore, Psalms 42-43 are teachings from David to help us learn how to handle our blue moods.

In the previous lesson, I mentioned a book by Martin Seligman titled *Learned Optimism*. In it, Seligman says that when we learn to be hopeless we tell ourselves three lies about the situation: We tell ourselves that what's going on is personal, pervasive, and permanent.[1] What he means is that when we are in despair, as David was, we tell ourselves things. David wanted to know why it felt as if God had forgotten him. We take our struggles *personally*.

Then, Seligman explains, we tell ourselves our struggles are pervasive, meaning this one thing that's wrong in our lives has affected everything else. But this assessment is not likely true, and though there might be one little corner of our lives that is messy, our whole lives may not be.

And then the worst lie that we tell ourselves is that everything happening is *permanent*. It's awful, it's bad, and it's never going to get better, especially if we've allowed ourselves to believe God has abandoned us. By the time we've got these lies in our heads, we're hopeless and helpless.

In this lesson we're going to look at David's experience with hopelessness in terms of the clues we can find in Psalms 42-43. We need to learn from him so we can avoid the traps of personalization, pervasiveness, and permanence when it comes to the temptation to lose hope. God never abandons His children, but if we don't continue to learn hopefulness through the recitation and review of biblical truth, we will find ourselves open to hopelessness.

Let's look at three paradoxes I find in these two psalms—seeming contradictions that arise during times of trouble.

HOPE IS MOST ALIVE WHEN EVERYTHING SEEMS HOPELESS

The first paradox is this: Hope is most alive when everything seems hopeless. Despair lurks behind hope the way the dark side of the moon lurks behind its shining face. Hope answers despair the way the sun answers the darkness of the night. The man who just lost his job, the woman whose husband has left, or the couple whose baby has a birth defect—all of them share similar feelings of despair. But the Word of God tells us that true hope always springs from despair.

Paul wrote in Romans 8:24-25 that the best time for hope to appear is when we cannot see hope: "For we were saved in this hope, but hope that is seen is not hope; for why does one still hope for what he sees? But if we hope for what we do not see, we eagerly wait for *it* with perseverance." If we see our hope, it's no longer hope. If you already have that for which you hope, you don't hope for it anymore because you already possess it. But hope you can't see causes you to persevere in hoping for it. There is a sense that if you want to have hope there has to be a place where it fits, and hope fits best where there is hopelessness. Simply put, if you already have hope then you don't need hope. But for the person who is in the situation David is in, who seems to have lost all hope for his life and his future, hope springs alive in a context of hopelessness!

But not just the Word of God teaches that. The medical experts tell us that's true. An article I read stated that hope begins when personal resources are exhausted. Studies have found that the most important ingredient needed to survive the Nazi death camps was blind, naked hope which was defined as being the kind of hope a person has to have when humanly speaking he can see no reason to hope at all. Hope is most alive when everything seems hopeless.

Listen to David's words in his situation:
- His soul was cast down and disturbed (42:5-6, 11; 43:5)
- He wept day and night; he lived on his tears (42:3)
- His soul was poured out within him (42:4)
- Waves of trouble were washing over him (42:7)
- He believed God had forgotten him (42:9; 43:2)
- He was oppressed by His enemies (42:9; 43:2)
- He felt like his bones were being broken (42:10)
- His enemies accused his God of abandoning him (42:10)

These are the words of a man whose spirit is broken and who feels hopeless about his situation. He feels ridiculed. He looks around, and even God seems to have abandoned him. But these psalms are about hope—because hope springs forth from despair.

It's important to remember that it is possible for serious, committed Christians to feel the emotions of depression and despair. It's not always the result of sin in your life as evidenced by David's situation. We have to look for that and see if it is there, but just being in a dark place doesn't automatically mean you've sinned. I'm reminded of Moses, a fugitive from justice, wandering in the desert, old and forgotten, discouraged. I'm reminded of godly Hannah, downhearted, unable to eat, a victim of hurtful remarks because she couldn't have children. And think of Paul with his "thorn" and Jesus with the cup of crucifixion He had to drink—they were in difficult and despairing places, but not because they had sinned. Sometimes life and its problems overwhelm us.

The great British preacher Charles Spurgeon suffered from prolonged bouts of depression as well as anxiety about all sorts of common problems, including finances. His psychological and physical ailments were so crippling that he frequently was confined to bed for weeks at a time. However, Spurgeon said that he came to see these problems as part of God's working in his life. His sufferings enabled him to comfort and encourage those who were similarly afflicted. He later wrote:

> Depression actually became a sort of John the Baptist for me. Just as John the Baptist came as a forerunner of Christ, my depression came as a forerunner to God's blessing in my life. When I would go through those terrible times of discouragement and depression and work through them, I always knew that right on the other side of that, God was going to do something great in my life.

Leith Anderson, in *A Church for the 21st Century* has written:

> Baby boomers desperately need hope. The church that reaches this generation definitely will be a church where hope is frequently dispensed. However, it is important that the church offer real, not contrived, hope. The kind of hope promised by the success gospel is looked on with a deserved cynicism by most baby boomers. Similarly, the hope offered by sincere, but unrealistic Christians, which ignores real pain and suffering, will not help disillusioned baby boomers. This generation will not respond to religious platitudes and clichés that minimize the hurt found in a fallen world. The church that offers hope will proclaim the God of Joseph, and Daniel, and Elijah and others like him. It will reveal a God who does not always remove us from our crises, but who always supports us in the midst of them, and brings us through them.[3]

Hope isn't the absence of all problems and difficulty. Hope is the knowledge that in the midst of them, God is there! Hope is the knowledge that we can put our trust in Him.

HOPE FOR THE FUTURE IS BUILT ON THE PAST

The first paradox is that hope springs from hopeless situations, and the second paradox is that hope for the future is built on the past.

"Hope" is a forward-thinking word. Say the word "hope" and you don't think about the past; you always think about the future. But when looking at Psalms 42-43, you can't help but notice how many times David referred to remembering and meditating. "When I remember these things, I pour out my soul within me. For I used to go with the multitude; I went with them to the house of God, with the voice of joy and praise, with a multitude that kept a pilgrim feast" (42:4).

When King David found himself in a place of discouragement, he began to remember the excitement of his spiritual life in Jerusalem as the king. He began to remember the history of the greatness of the God he serves. Psalm 77 gives us a similar prayer to what David might have said in his thoughts: "And I said, 'This is my anguish; But I will remember the years of the right hand of the Most High.' I will remember the works of the Lord; surely I will remember Your wonders of old" (verses 10-11).

One of the things that happens to us when we get discouraged is we forget what's already happened in the past. We forget to look back and count our blessings and remember how good God has been to us. All we can think of is how we are going to get through to the future, and we forget that the God of the past who has served us well is also the God of the future.

You may recall the incident in David's life before he ascended to the throne when he and his soldiers left their families in a city called Ziklag. They returned from a battle to discover that the city had been burned to the ground and all their wives were furious with him. They had given him their allegiance only to lose all their possessions and their families.

But instead of falling into the pit of despair, "David encouraged himself in the Lord his God" (1 Samuel 30:6). When you get discouraged, when you feel hopeless, don't just sit there and let it roll over you like the billows and waves. You've got to learn how to encourage your heart in the Lord. And one of the ways you do that is by going back through the Scriptures and remembering the greatness of God. If you keep a journal (you are keeping a journal, aren't you?), go back maybe a few months and read some of the pages where God was doing marvelous things in your life. God hasn't changed! The God who was the God of your hope in the past is the God of your hope now.

HOPE SINGS WHEN IT FEELS LIKE CRYING

The third paradox we find in David's experience is that hope sings when it feels like crying. The psalmist ends his Psalm by singing. We read, "I shall yet praise Him, who is the help of my countenance and my God" (Psalm 42:11b; 43:5b).

In my estimation, one of the hopeful signs of the American church is the recovery of the lost art of congregational involvement in worship. In recent years there has been a renewal, a renaissance, a recovery of participation in worshiping God. And that's not only good for us as the Church, and not only a blessing to God who hears our corporate praise, but that is one of the healthiest things we can all do for our moods when we feel despair as David did.

David planned on returning to his worshipful ways as evidenced by his words in Psalm 43:4 when he said, "Then I will go to the altar of God, to God my exceeding joy; and on the harp I will praise You, O God, my God." Even in the nighttime he expected God's song to be with him (42:8). Some people say discouragement and depression are worse at night. But even David remembered songs of worship and praise to God. He said, "God gave me a song in the night."

When you sing, it's impossible to imagine the greatness of God and think about your own misery at the same time. When you begin to worship and praise God, you become very much aware of His magnificent greatness, and suddenly the things that are going on in your life begin to pale to insignificance when you see them in comparison to God. There's something about music, about the melodic strains, that captures your emotions and brings them captive again to God.

Don Wyrtzen, a very gifted composer, pianist, and writer, has written a little book called *A Musician Looks at the Book of Psalms*— devotionals on the psalms through the eyes of a musician like David himself. Concerning Psalm 42, Wyrtzen wrote:

> Dark moods can give way to positive praying. Like the Psalmist, I can't allow my mind to camp on negative ideas and feelings, but I can pray for God's light and truth to guide me. Let them bring me to Your holy mountain, to the place

where You dwell. In the sanctuary, in the presence of my fellow believers, I will praise the Lord with acoustic and electric instruments, with sophisticated rhythms, with innovative harmonies and soaring melodies, all reveling in the ineffable glory of God. In this way, I, too, will be able to experience His transforming power.[4]

There is an interesting variation in David's words that may reflect the power of praise on his life. In Psalm 42:5 he wrote, "I shall yet praise Him for the help of *His* countenance" (italics added). But in verse 11 he wrote, "I shall yet praise *Him*, the help of *my* countenance and my God" (italics added). On the one hand he praised God for God's countenance, and on the other he praised God for God's impact on his own countenance. D. Martyn Lloyd-Jones says the psalmist is telling us that "When I really look at God, as I get better, my face gets better."[5]

If the face is a mirror of the soul, then that becomes a pretty good reason to sing the praises of God. Our countenance reflects the changing condition of our soul as we praise God.

Have you noticed the inscription at the beginning of Psalm 42? The inscriptions were part of the original text of the psalm in its role in the hymnbook of Israel. The inscription of Psalm 42 says it was, "To the Chief Musician. A contemplation of the sons of Korah." It's a teaching psalm to "the sons of Korah." But who were they?

The story of Korah is in Numbers 16—a sad tale of rebellion against the leadership of Moses and Aaron as the redeemed Hebrew slaves made their way from Egypt to Canaan. Korah rebelled and convinced others to follow him, and God responded with judgment. The ground opened up and swallowed Korah and his followers, their households and their possessions. The rebellion was halted in short order.

Although the adults were removed for rebelling, the children weren't killed. The children were spared. If you had known any of those children or their legacy, you would have been thinking, "There's no hope for them."

The descendants "sons" of Korah went on to become the Levitical singers in the temple worship in Jerusalem. God took those hopeless children and turned them into worship leaders! Out of the ash heap of the broken promises and rebellion of their parents, God raised up as a testimony to hope, generation after generation of children who stood in the presence of God in the sanctuary and blessed His holy name.

Our God is a God of hope. He can take the thing that looks the most hopeless to you and out of that, raise a testimony to His own name.

If you feel hopeless, you're a candidate for hope—you are in the perfect place to see hope arise out of your dark place. If you want to encourage your heart in the Lord, begin to review what God has done for you in the past and enter into a time of worship and praise. As you start to praise your God, you'll find hope. Remember: At the time you feel least hopeful, that is when hope is most likely to appear.

Notes:

1. Martin E. P. Seligman, *Learned Optimism* (New York: A. A. Knopf, 1991), 43-51.

2. Warren Wiersbe, *Walking with the Giants* (Grand Rapids: Baker Book House, 1980).

3. Leith Anderson, *A Church for the 21st Century* (Minneapolis: Bethany House Publishers, 1992).

4. Don Wyrtzen, *A Musician Looks at the Psalms* (Nashville: Broadman & Holman Publishers, 2004), 131.

5. David Martyn Lloyd-Jones, *Spiritual Depression: Its Causes and Cure* (Grand Rapids: Eerdmans, 1965), 13.

1. Read Psalm 42-43.

    a. When David's soul was cast down, what does he remember? (42:6) What areas of your life may cause you to be cast down?

    b. When David is distressed, instead of falling into the pit of despair, what does he do? (1 Samuel 30:6) What's an example in your life of when you gave in to despair instead of turning to the Lord? How can this verse reassure you to turn to the Lord in desperate times, instead?

c. What does David ask of God in Psalm 43:1b? What does the word *vindicate* mean, and why is it important in this context? What can you ask the Lord to vindicate you of?

d. What is the significance of "yet" in Psalms 42:11b and 43:5b? Why is it important to praise God, even in your suffering (43:4)?

2. Read Psalm 77:1-20.

   a. What was the psalmist's condition? (verses 1-2a) What did he do in response to his situation? (verse 2) Can you remember a time when your soul was troubled and you felt like God wasn't listening?

   b. How would you answer the questions that the psalmist asked himself in verses 7-9? What does he choose to remember after asking and answering these questions? (verses 10-11)

1. Read Romans 8:18-30.

   a. Discuss some examples in history that seemed hopeless, but the people survived because they didn't give up hope. What are some examples today?

   b. What does Paul say will be waiting for Christians after they endure the suffering of this present time? (verses 18-19)

   c. What are some current world issues that cause people to feel hopeless? How can Christians respond?

d. According to this lesson, "hope is most alive when everything seems hopeless." Does the apostle Paul agree with this statement (verses 24-25)? Share a time in your life when everything seemed hopeless but God came through for you.

e. In times of despair, what is needed to survive? How does this lesson use the example of the Holocaust victims to prove this point?

f. Examine the importance of remembering God's character and the value of His promises in times of hopelessness. Do you feel like the world has lost its hope? How can this be fixed?

2. According to Matthew 5:13-16, what is a Christian's objective on earth?

3. Share plausible ideas on how this goal may be fulfilled.

4. Discuss ideas on how to deal with tragic times and how to hold on to hope when times are at their worst.

5. What are some ways that you can strengthen your hope in Christ?

DID YOU KNOW?

Even though Psalms 42-43 are separate psalms in our modern Bibles, most scholars believe that they were originally parts of the same psalm. The themes of both psalms are obviously the same, and the refrains in 42:5, 11, and 43:5 are identical. The beginning verse of Psalm 42 (a longing for God) and the penultimate verse of Psalm 43 (a vow to return to the altar to praise God) provide obvious bookends for a single psalm. Plus, Psalm 43 has no inscription preceding verse 1 as if the inscription of Psalm 42 was for both when they were a single psalm.

A LIVING HOPE

1 Peter 1

*In this lesson we discover the uniqueness
of the living hope found in Christ.*

OUTLINE

There is hope and there is living hope. In the world, hope is a
synonym for "wish" ("I hope it rains tomorrow"). From God's
perspective, living hope is synonymous with the living Christ.
When Christ conquered death through the Resurrection, He became
the source of living hope.

   I.   **Our Living Hope Is in the Person of Christ**

  II.   **Our Living Hope Is Eternal**

 III.   **Our Living Hope Is Sure**

 IV.   **Our Living Hope Is Daily**

The world today is reeling through a spectrum of disillusionment. Every day the news greets us with yet another disaster, another reminder of how far the world has fallen and all of the things that can cause us to lose hope. As we are studying the subject of hope, it has become apparent to all of us that there are an awful lot of people seeking for answers, and there aren't many people finding them.

But here's the good news: We as Christians know God and His Son Jesus Christ, and we don't have to be left at the corner of Hopelessness and Despair. There is an answer to everything, and it is Jesus.

There is a writer of a New Testament book who understood this truth completely and wrote it down for us so we would never doubt its reality. His name is Peter. In the first chapter of his first epistle, he makes an important statement about the nature of hope. The Christians Peter was writing to were facing untold persecution and suffering during the time when Rome was in its tyranny against believers. In this one epistle, Peter makes reference to suffering sixteen times. He wanted the suffering Christians to understand that Christ would carry them through. He wrote about the "living hope."

OUR LIVING HOPE IS IN THE PERSON OF CHRIST

Peter has a good word for us about how we are to face suffering, and it's wrapped around hope. He tells us that we can have hope if we will understand and believe the truth concerning the risen Christ. In the third verse of the first chapter he says it this way: "Blessed be the God and Father of our Lord Jesus Christ, who according to His abundant mercy has begotten us again to a living hope through the resurrection of Jesus Christ from the dead."

Peter would have us believe in no uncertain language that the hope for which we seek and often eludes us is to be found in a Person who has overcome death. There is one certain reason for having hope regardless of the way the world or our life is going, and that reason is named Jesus!

I can't help but think when Peter wrote these words about the living hope in the resurrected Christ, perhaps his own personal experience had come back to him. Peter had been a close friend of the Lord's and walked with Him through most of His public ministry.

And he had some problems. He denied the Lord three times and had to go through the process of being recommissioned as a disciple. That's why all of us like Peter so much. He gives us a sense of identity. We believe that if he could make it with the Lord, maybe we could, too. But in the end, Peter loved the Lord, and he had great hope that Jesus was their Messiah who would come and free them from Roman bondage. Peter pinned his hopes on Him.

Then one day it started—the anger, the accusations, the mock trial, the beating, the crown of thorns, the cross, the journey up the hill, the spear, the nails, and the end. And everything Peter had believed in and everything he had hoped for was taken down off of that cross, wrapped in linen, and laid in a rock hewn tomb. Peter did not understand why Jesus was killed—his hopes for the restoration of Israel were dashed.

And then one day, word started to spread that the tomb was empty. But Peter had to see for himself. So he ran with John, and saw the garments by themselves and the reality of the Resurrection began to take root in his heart. And the moment when he saw Him for the first time, and examined the nail prints in His hands and the place where the spear had gone into His side, it was an overwhelming feeling for Peter to realize this One whom he had seen die had come out of the grave. He was alive! He was the risen Lord!

It is that background Peter calls on when he wrote to those early Christians who were suffering for their faith. He wrote to them and said, "I want to tell you something. You have a living hope. And that hope is based upon what Jesus Christ did when He came out of the grave. He promises to those who put their faith in Him that they, too, shall overcome death."

So Peter is telling you if you are looking for hope, it is found in Jesus Christ. Think about this: What do you say to a woman who finds out that she has a disease that is going to take her life, that her days have been numbered? If all we ever have to say to one another in our hopelessness and disillusionment is temporal, earthly things we are left without anything to hang on to. Paul wrote about this to the Corinthians: "If in this life only we have hope, we are of all men most pitiable" (1 Corinthians 15:19). The hope the world can offer ends at the grave.

Peter says our living hope is found in the person of the Lord Jesus Christ because we can pin our hope on Him. He is the only one who ever did what He did. Jesus, the Messiah, the Christ, defeated man's greatest enemy by coming back from death alive and victorious. And His promise is this: If you put your trust in Him, as He lives, you too shall live. That is why when we stand by the casket of a loved one who has died in Christ, we have living hope. We shed tears of sorrow at the person's absence, but not tears of despair. Why? Because we have a living hope! We know we will be reunited with the person from whom we are temporarily separated.

There are three things about living hope that make it different from the "hope" offered by the world: it is eternal, it is sure, and it is daily.

OUR LIVING HOPE IS ETERNAL

No matter how dark the situations in our lives might become, our hope is anchored in Jesus Christ and in His power over death. Paul told the Corinthian believers that if this were not true we don't have faith and we're still in our sin, still hopeless.

The reality of this hope hit home when I read an article by a friend of mine. She is a woman who is no stranger to tragedy and difficulty. Her name is Joni Eareckson Tada. Many know how she was paralyzed from the neck down in a teenage diving accident. In her book, *Heaven: Your Real Home*, Eareckson tells a story that illustrates the power of hope in this life. Since she is paralyzed and can't feel pain, the only way she knows something is wrong is based on learned feelings: her temperature and blood pressure go up, and she has an intuitive sensation that something is wrong. With the aid of an assistant, she has to look to see if she has injured herself in some way. I'll quote from her book:

> My face flushed and my eyes became damp. For the fourth time that day, I needed to be lifted out of my wheelchair and laid down, I had to undress to readjust my corset—shallow breathing, sweating, and a sky-rocketing blood pressure were signaling that something was either pinching, bruising, or sticking my paralyzed body. My secretary tissued away my tears and unfolded my office sofa bed.

> As she shifted my body, examining my legs and hips for any telltale pressure marks or red areas, I stared vacantly at the ceiling, "I want to quit this," I mumbled. We couldn't find anything wrong. . .

> I looked sheepish. "Where do I go to resign from this stupid paralysis?". . .

> As she gathered the pile of letters off my desk, and was about to leave, she paused and leaned against the door. "I bet you can't wait for heaven. You know, like Paul said, 'We groan, longing to be clothed with a heavenly dwelling.'"

My eyes dampened again, but this time they were tears of relief and hope. "Yeah, it'll be great."

I sat and dreamed what I've dreamed of a thousand times: the hope of heaven. I jerked my will right side up, refocused my emotions, and realigned my thoughts. I mentally rehearsed a flood of other promises and fixed the eyes of my heart on unseen divine realities and future divine fulfillments. I zeroed in on a few heavenly coordinates to lift my sights above my physical pain: When we see Him we shall be like Him. The perishable shall put on the imperishable—the corruptible, that which is incorruptible. That which is sown in weakness will be raised in power. He has given us an inheritance that can never perish, spoil or fade. If we suffer with Him, we shall reign with Him. It was all I needed. I opened my eyes and said out loud with a smile, "Come quickly, Lord Jesus."[1]

Christian hope isn't just pie-in-the-sky hope to masquerade or camouflage our current difficulties. It is not "hope-so-hope," it is "know-so-hope." This is knowing the One who has done what no one else has ever done. And by virtue of having done that, Jesus has laid claim to our faith and told us that since He came out of the grave victorious over death, we can trust in Him and have the same victory.

OUR LIVING HOPE IS SURE

In 1 Peter 1:4, Peter writes that our inheritance in Christ is "incorruptible and undefiled" and will not "fade away," that it is "reserved in heaven" for us. That sounds like a sure thing, far more sure than anything in which we can place our trust on this earth.

When I was a seminary student in Dallas, Texas, I got caught up in the Dallas Cowboys. I went to their Tuesday luncheons. I read every sports page about what was going on and I knew everything that was happening with every player. Once, when a home game failed to sell out, and the local broadcast of the game was blacked out on TV, my wife and I drove to Oklahoma and checked into a motel so we could watch the game on TV!

But this is what I discovered about following a sports team: I didn't feel any better when they won than I did when they lost. Sure, I was excited for a moment or two, but then I had to ask, "So what?"

I'm not suggesting that we shouldn't put our hope in and depend on one another in this life, or our bonding together in families shouldn't be strong. But there is a hope even more important than that, and that is the hope we place in the eternal God through His Son Jesus Christ. He is the source of true hope that the world can never offer.

OUR LIVING HOPE IS DAILY

You say, "Is the living hope we have in Christ for the future only? Does it only satisfy the hope I have for eternal life? How is my relationship with Jesus Christ going to make any difference in my life now?" First Peter 1:5 says, "[You] who are kept by the power of God through faith for salvation ready to be revealed in the last time."

In verse 4, Peter says that God has given us a hope that is secure and steadfast, it can't ever be touched. It is beyond decay and destruction. Nothing can ever happen to it. And in the next verse (verse 5), He says God is committed to keeping us on our way to the full realization of that hope. It is a day by day guarantee that in the process of our going to that ultimate realization of hope He is going to keep us safe. The word "kept" in verse 5 is one of the strongest words in the New Testament—it's a military term that means to be kept or made secure by a troop of soldiers. Peter is saying as you have fixed your eyes upon Jesus and put your trust in Him, then He has promised to keep you and help you every day.

The great Christian thinker C. S. Lewis wrote, "Aim at heaven and you will get earth thrown in: aim at earth, you will get neither."[2] That is a powerful truth. What he is saying is this: If you don't get heaven straight, you won't get there, but in the process of not getting there, you won't have anything worth living for down here. It is only by having our anchor planted firmly in heaven that we get hope and security for this life.

In verse 6 Peter admits that, in this life, we might be "grieved by various trials." And he's absolutely correct. But that doesn't mean the status of our living hope is changed. Quite the contrary: Our living hope is proven to be genuine (like gold in the refiner's fire) when we pass through "various trials" (verse 7). He's saying put your hope in the Lord and get ready for some challenges. There are going to be manifest trials in your life that will buffet you, but even in the process of the trials God has a purpose.

A Scottish theologian by the name of Samuel Rutherford explains the purpose of these problems we face in the midst of our life of hope. Joni Eareckson Tada quoted these words in connection with her own disability:

> If God had told me some time ago that he was about to make me as happy as I could be in this world, and then had told me that he should begin by crippling me in arm or limb or

removing me from all my usual sources of enjoyment, I should have thought it a very strange mode of accomplishing his purpose. And yet, how is his wisdom manifest even in this? For if you should see a man shut up in a dark room, idolizing a set of lamps and rejoicing in their light, and you wish to make him truly happy, you would begin by blowing out all of his lamps and then throw open the shutters to let in the light of heaven.[3]

And here is Eareckson's response in light of her own situation:

That's exactly what God did for me when He sent a broken neck my way. He blew out the lamps in my life that lit up the here and now and made it so captivating. The dark despair of total and permanent paralysis that followed wasn't much fun, but it sure made heaven come alive. And one day, when our Bridegroom comes back—probably when I'm right in the middle of lying down on my office sofa for the umpteenth time—God is going to throw open heaven's shutters. There's not a doubt in my mind that I'll be fantastically more excited and ready for it than if I were on my feet.[4]

Christians and non-Christians have an equal number of hurts and disappointments in this life. But there is a vast difference in the way we process these disappointments. A Christian has superficial sorrow and central gladness; a non-Christian has superficial gladness and central sorrow. An unbeliever without hope resorts to superficial gladness to cover his emptiness when circumstances reveal a lack of hope. A believer maintains his core perspective of hope.

One of my favorite people in the world of Christian music is Bill Gaither. He, along with his wife Gloria, have given the church a treasure-trove of beautiful Gospel songs. In her book *Because He Lives*, Gloria tells of a particularly discouraging period in their lives back in the early 1960s. Bill had just been through a bout of mononucleosis and Gloria was pregnant with one of their children. She tells how, looking around at the chaotic state of America and the world in the Sixties, she despaired over bringing a child into such a world. Everything seemed so dangerous and out-of-control, she worried about their decision to have a baby.

But one day the Lord ministered to her in her area of concern and helped her understand that life in Christ is a secure hope against all the instability the world might produce, that there was nothing to fear for those whose living hope was Christ Himself. She began to express new-found thoughts of confidence in God on paper, and the song "Because He Lives" was the ultimate result: "Because He loves, I can face tomorrow. Because He lives, all fear is gone. Because I know He holds the future, and life is worth the living just because He lives."

It's in the second verse that we see Gloria's renewed hope at a personal level: "How sweet to hold our newborn baby, and feel the pride and joy He gives. But greater still the calm assurance, our child can face uncertain days because He lives."[5]

Not long after that song was written, Bill's father was visiting them at their music publishing office. He came in one day and asked Bill and Gloria to go with him to the parking lot so he could show them something. Just a few months prior, the parking lot had been repaved: a layer of stone pressed down, then a layer of pea gravel pressed down, then a layer of hot, molten asphalt pressed down. And there, up through the rock and the pea gravel and the asphalt was a tiny green shoot that had sprung up. It didn't come up because it was strong or because it was sharp. It came up through that molten asphalt because it had one quality, and that is because it was alive. Life always reigns over that where there is no life.

Life makes all the difference! And it makes a difference in the hope we have as Christians and the so-called end-at-the-grave hope that the world has to offer. When the rocks and gravel and hot asphalt of this world attempt to bury us, our living hope springs eternal and bears fruit in spite of the circumstances.

If you have never put your hope in God, you need to make that decision because that is where it begins. There is no other hope besides His that is eternal, sure, and sufficient for your daily needs.

Notes:

1. Joni Eareckson Tada, Heaven: Your Real Home (Grand Rapids: Zondervan, 1996), 168-169.

2. C. S. Lewis, *Mere Christianity* (New York: Collier, 1960), 118.

3. Quoted in Joni Eareckson Tada, *Heaven: Your Real Home* (Grand Rapids: Zondervan, 1996), 177.

4. Tada, p. 177

5. Gloria Gaither, *Because He Lives* (Old Tappan: Fleming H. Revell, 1977), 173-175.

1. Read 1 Peter 1.

   a. What circumstances were the Christians under when Peter wrote this epistle?

   b. According to verse 3, how are you able to have a "living hope"? What's an example of a time when you were attacked for being a Christian?

   c. Is the Living Hope you have in Christ for the future, or is it worked out daily in your life as you journey toward heaven? (verse 5)

d. What does Peter tell us we may face in this life? (verse 6)

e. Why might this happen and what will be the outcome? (verses 7 and 8) List troubles you've had beyond persecution for your faith.

f. What is the significance of the word "Therefore" in verse 13?

g. Look back through verses 1-12 and identify the reasons for the statement in verse 13. Reflect on how you can respond to hardship, according to this verse.

h. How is conforming to the world and the flesh (verse 14) an evidence of a loss of hope in the return of Christ?

i. Why is remembering God's character and His promises valuable in times of hopelessness?

j. Explain the critical role Christ plays in the plan of God and for restoring faith and hope in the hearts of human beings. (verses 17-21) Who can you pray for who needs faith and hope in God (be it someone in the government, close family, etc.)?

k. In what ways has knowing Christ given you hope? Why are you able to have hope even in the midst of troubles?

1. Read 1 Peter 1.

   a. Discuss Peter's description of Christian's inheritance in Christ (verse 4).

   b. We may not understand God's purpose but we must believe His promises. Discuss Joni's story about finding light through her paralysis. What was a time in your life when God showed you His light by removing you from your comfort zone?

   c. What's the difference between a Christian's and a non-Christian's sorrow and gladness?

d. What do "girding up one's mind" and being "sober" have to do with "setting one's hope"? (verse 13). Share ideas on how to follow those instructions.

e. The Berean Study Bible states, "Therefore, prepare your minds for action" (verse13). What action do you think this translation refers to?

f. Why is being delivered from "aimless conduct" a reason for hope (verse 18)? What, in life, could be considered "aimless"?

g. Do you think it's important to surround yourselves with Christians in times of hardship? Why? Does the Bible give any examples of this?

h. Read and discuss the following Scriptures. What truth is found in each reference?

• Isaiah 43:1-3

• Psalm 34:4-8

• 1 Peter 5:7-10

DID YOU KNOW?

It is thought by most scholars that the persecution to which Peter makes reference (1 Peter 4:14-16; 5:8-9) occurred during the reign of Emperor Nero, the last of the line of Julius Caesar. The first years of Nero's reign (A.D. 54-63) were years of peace and order in the Roman Empire. The apostle Paul was brought before Nero in A.D. 63 without recrimination. But in A.D. 64, a large part of Rome burned, and Nero used Christians as a scapegoat, inflicting widespread suffering. He ultimately took his own life in A.D. 68, but not before executing the apostles Paul and Peter.

HOPE IN THE VALLEY OF TROUBLE

Joshua 7; Hosea 2:15

In this lesson we learn how a place of trouble can become a place of hope.

OUTLINE

Trouble can come our way for many reasons, not the least of which is our choices that are inconsistent with God's will. When that happens, the best thing we can do is take action to correct our choices in order to regain our hope and peace. It's always possible for hope to be restored.

I. **How We Can Lose Our Hope**
   A. Through God's Actions in Our Lives
   B. Through the Actions of Others
   C. Through Self-Inflicted Spiritual Injury

II. **How We Can Regain Our Hope**
   A. Decide to Take Action
   B. Get to the Core of the Problem
   C. Don't Rationalize What You Find
   D. Deal With the Problem Honestly Before God
   E. Destroy the Barrier That Is Keeping You From Hope

Y ou may be familiar with, or even have read, the books by Dave Dravecky, the Major League Baseball pitcher who developed cancer in his throwing arm. After some time away for treatment, he made a dramatic comeback and pitched again before having to leave the game he loved.

Comeback was the first book that told the story of his cancer and return to the game. His second book, *When You Can't Come Back*, written with his wife, Jan, told a more sobering story of his life after his dream was permanently shattered. In the second book he wrote:

> Ever since the first game with my dad, baseball had been my life. And my life as a ball player was wrapped up in my arm. The more strikes that my arm could throw, the more I was worth. The more games that arm won, the more managers wanted me on their teams.
>
> "How's the arm today, Dave?" "Is your arm ready for tonight?" "Better get some ice on that arm. Don't want it to swell up."
>
> My arm was to me what hands are to a pianist, what legs are to a ballerina. It's what the fans cheered for, what they paid hard-earned money to see. It was what gave me worth, at least in the eyes of the world.[1]
>
> In January of 1990, my wife, Jan, and I left for Memorial Sloan Kettering Cancer Center in New York City where Dr. Murray Brennan found that the tumor in my pitching arm had returned. He removed the rest of my deltoid muscle plus 10 percent of my triceps, and isolated me for five days of treatment with iridium pellets. God had stood by me before, but now He seemed to be withdrawing. It really scared me.[2]
>
> By May, the cancer had wrapped itself around my radial nerve. Dr. Brennan scraped the nerve of cancerous cells, but the prognosis wasn't good. My doubleheader with cancer was going into extra innings.
>
> In July and August, I underwent further radiation treatment. Shortly afterward I began to run a low-grade fever, and my doctor discovered a staph infection in my arm. I fought the pain and the persistent infection until one day when Jan and I visited an elementary school. I spoke to some sixty kids and showed them a video of my comeback game, the game in Montreal where I broke my arm. The kids flocked around me

with scraps of paper and baseball cards for me to sign. As I tried to sign those cards, I pushed through the loops and curves of my name and my arm was almost immobile. I finally realized: it was time. It was time to face what I really never had wanted to face before. It was time to face the loss of my left arm.[3]

We'll come back to Dave Dravecky's story in a moment. I want to remind you of another contest. This one was not an athletic event. It was an international conflict on the battlefield. The battle of Jericho.

Joshua had been commissioned by God to invade Canaan, take the cities, and drive out the inhabitants. Jericho was a walled city on the west bank of the Jordan River, Joshua's first obstacle as the Israelites entered Canaan. God gave Joshua an unusual battle plan for capturing Jericho. They marched around the walls, and on the last day they blew their trumpets and shouted with loud voices, and God brought the walls crumbling down. Joshua and the army of Israel rejoiced greatly at the victory. If they could keep this up, taking Canaan would be no problem.

What happened next we often see happen in life today, especially in athletic events. After this great victory, Israel got a bit arrogant and cocky. They didn't have to lift a sword to capture Jericho, so they believed taking their next target, Ai, would be simple. Again, Joshua sent a reconnaissance team to spy on Ai; when they returned, they told Joshua, "Do not let all the people go up, but let about two or three thousand men go up and attack Ai. Do not weary all the people there, for *the people of Ai are few*" (7:3).

That would be the equivalent of a basketball team saying, "Let's only take four guys to the next game. Any four of us can beat any five of them." Or a football team leaving all of its reserve players at home and just going with enough people. Israel had forgotten that the victory had nothing to do with the number of people they had. It had everything to do with their trust and dependence upon God.

So Joshua listened to the spies and sent 3,000 men to Ai, and they were soundly defeated. Instead of defeating Ai, the Israelites were chased out of the city and 36 lost their lives. What Joshua didn't know was something else was going on underneath the surface that caused their defeat. There was sin in the camp. But not knowing this at the time, Joshua and the people responded with shock, anger, disappointment, and discouragement. "The hearts of the people melted and became like water" (verse 5). Suddenly the victory over Jericho was forgotten and they were afraid again.

Joshua got angry with God. He and the elders tore their clothes and threw dust on their heads—a sign of grief and mourning—and Joshua cried out to God: "Alas, Lord GOD, why have You brought this people over the Jordan at all—to deliver us into the hands of the Amorites, to destroy us? Oh, that we had been content, and dwelt on the other side of the Jordan! O Lord, what shall I say when Israel turns its back before its enemies?" (verses 7-8)

Joshua and the people had lost their hope in God, but their hope was restored. That's the lesson we want to learn from their experience.

How We Can Lose Our Hope

There are three ways we can lose our hope, and we need to be aware of them all.

Through God's Actions in Our Lives

We've been talking about hope, and we've learned already that sometimes we lose our hope for a brief time because of what God is doing in our lives. Sometimes He is working on us, and if we are not careful, we won't understand what is going on. This can cause us to lose our sense of hope. But God working on us should not devastate us. When God is working on us in our lives with one hand, and He is doing it to build us up and strengthen us, He's always using the other hand to encourage us and help us through the process.

Through the Actions of Others

Sometimes we get confused in our hope, not because of what God is doing, but because of what others are doing to us. There are people in the world who do bad things. But Scripture tells us that when somebody is mistreating us, we can still go to God and He vindicates us. He vindicates the innocent and the just, so we can go to Him and He will give us comfort and encouragement. God knows our hearts, and if we are innocent in His eyes we have no reason to despair.

Through Self-Inflicted Spiritual Injury

The third way we can lose our hope is the most important, and that is through our own self-inflicted spiritual injury. In my estimation, this is the most devastating of the three. There are countless people in the Church who have lost the joy in their hearts not because God is working on them and not because they have been mistreated by others, but because they took a turn when God told them to go straight. They have self-inflicted pain and injury in their hearts and it's caused them to lose hope.

People have described it to me like this: "You know, Pastor Jeremiah, I don't know what it is, but there is something just not right in my life. I feel like I'm somehow out of sync a little bit. I love God, and I know I'm a Christian, but sometimes when I lie in bed in the morning, I just know that there is something not the way it should be. I don't have the enthusiasm to serve God that I once had. I don't have the sense of well-being that I had when I began to walk with the Lord. There is something wrong. I've lost my hope."

That's what was going on when the men of Israel went up against Ai. Somewhere in the process they realized something was wrong. Something had happened. And Joshua sensed the Israelites had something to do with it. So what do you do when you sense that your hope has begun to fade and you had something to do with it?

HOW WE CAN REGAIN OUR HOPE

In Joshua's story we'll find five principles, five steps, for restoring hope.

Decide to Take Action

The first step is to decide to fix the problem of hopelessness! The enemy of your soul wants to give you the impression that there is nothing you can do about where you are and how things are in your life. The way things are is the way they will always be. The enemy wants you to believe that you are unredeemable. If you believe him, you will never move forward. You must decide to do something about your hopelessness by seeking the Lord to discover the reason for the situation.

Joshua fell on his face before the Lord and, truth be told, was having a sort of pity-party, complaining that his army was defeated by Ai. And right at the moment when Joshua was whining the loudest and ringing his hands the hardest, the Lord spoke (and none too gently): "Get up! Why do you lie thus on your face?" (verse 10). Joshua was crying, complaining, and feeling sorry for himself, and God told him to stop!

After telling Joshua to get up, God said: "Get up, sanctify the people, and say, 'Sanctify yourselves for tomorrow . . .'" (verse 13). God wanted to meet with Joshua and the people to fix the mess they were in.

The enemy wants you to believe that where you are is where you have to stay. It's not true! So decide to take action as Joshua did.

Get to the Core of the Problem

In Joshua's day, warfare was a spiritual endeavor as much as a military one. It wasn't just how many men Israel had, it was about spiritual integrity, about whether they were walking with God or not.

You may already know the story of what they discovered. God had given clear instructions when they defeated Jericho that none of the property of Jericho was to be taken by Israelite soldiers. But a man named Achan rummaged around in one of the dwellings in Jericho after the walls had fallen, and took some gold and silver and buried it in the ground inside his tent. And because of that act of disobedience, God judged Israel with a defeat at the hands of Ai.

As we follow Joshua's story, we realize that he didn't know what the problem was. We know because we have the benefit of reading the story after the fact. But Joshua didn't know. So God put him on a path to find out. He was to follow the Lord's leading in winnowing out the guilty party (verse 14). The process was one of selecting the tribe (Judah), the clan (Judah), the family (the Zarhites), the household (Zabdi), and the individual perpetrator (Achan, son of Carmi) (verses 16-18).

With God's help, Joshua went from knowing nothing to knowing the individual who had sinned against the Lord. That is the principle God wants us to apply to our own lives when we discover we have lost hope because of something we are involved in. We must obediently follow God's guidance as He reveals the sin at the root of the problem so it may be dealt with.

We may be like Joshua at the outset—we may have no idea what the problem is. It may be in the realm of our family, a place where it is easy to walk around looking like everything is okay while violating family relationships. A husband or wife could be unhappy at home and begin to entertain notions of a relationship with someone outside of the marriage. Or maybe it has to do with finances. Maybe you are not being a good steward of what God has provided. You've stopped being generous and started being selfish.

You soon begin to understand why you wake up early in the morning thinking about life as it is in your own heart and you feel something's wrong. As you go through the winnowing and narrowing, the searchlight of God's Word zeroes in on what is going on, and soon you discover what has taken your hope.

There are many other categories of ordinary life in which we can stop obeying God and find ourselves defeated and hopeless.

But you decide to take action and then you go before God and say, "God, show me what it is." That's the prayer of David in Psalm 139: "Search me, O God, and know my heart . . . see if there is any wicked way in me" (verses 23-24). We must do what is necessary to get to the root of the problem.

Don't Rationalize What You Find

When God shows us a problem in our life, the immediate response is to justify ourselves or talk ourselves into feeling better about it than we should. Instead of calling sin what it is, we talk about cultural problems and the pressures of the generation in which we live. It's so hard for us, even after we identify the problem, to be able to say, "This is not good. This is in violation of the things of God and I need to deal with it."

When Joshua confronted Achan (verse 19), he asked Achan to "give glory to the LORD God of Israel, and make confession to Him," and say what he had done rather than hiding it. (Remember, Joshua still didn't know what Achan had done. He only knew Achan was guilty.)

Achan confessed his sin in detail, telling exactly what he had done (verse 20). He didn't rationalize or justify his sin. He didn't shift the blame to another person. He didn't feign ignorance to what God commanded. He simply owned up to what he had done.

Deal With the Problem Honestly Before God

Verse 23 describes what should be done after we identify the sin problem in our lives. "And they took [the idols] from the midst of the tent, brought them to Joshua and to all the children of Israel, and laid them out before the LORD."

It is not enough to admit what we did, nor is it enough to ask forgiveness of those we have harmed. Ultimately, our sin must be laid out "before the LORD." The children of Israel provide an example we can follow. They didn't try to hide from what God had revealed to them. They saw everything plainly and didn't run from what had to be done. They laid everything before God, telling Him they didn't like the feeling of being hopeless, they understood the problem. God isolated the problem and they saw it; they didn't rationalize anything. They simply laid it at His feet. God wants the same for us because until sin is confessed, it remains in the dark corners of our rationalizing mind.

Destroy the Barrier That Is Keeping You From Hope

Once we discover what the barrier is between God and ourselves, we must deal with it ruthlessly. We must remove it from our life so God's blessing and hope can return.

Achan's confession did not absolve him of his punishment. When Joshua was finished with Achan, verse 24 tells us that Israel took Achan, the property he had stolen, his family, his animals, and his possessions to the Valley of Achor (Valley of Trouble) where they were stoned and burned. As a result, "the LORD turned from the fierceness of His anger" (verse 26) and hope returned to Israel.

If God isolates the problem with your hope, and you know it's destroying your hope, deal with it ruthlessly and relentlessly. Get rid of it! I've had people tell me they know they are doing something they shouldn't and they're working through it. Sin should not be "worked through." It should be dealt with actively and decisively. As Joshua and the Israelites did, pile stones on it and burn it with the fire of your passion to see hope restored!

Hundreds of years after God judged Achan (and by extension, Israel) in the Valley of Achor, He said through the prophet Hosea, "I will give her...the Valley of Achor as a door of hope; she shall sing there, as in the days of her youth, as in the day when she came up from the land of Egypt" (Hosea 2:15). Israel sinned, dealt with the sin, and so God was able to open a door of hope in the same place. And the same will be true in our lives if we will destroy the barrier that keeps us from hope.

Dave Dravecky found hope in his own Valley of Trouble. He discovered that God is sufficient reason to have a heart filled with hope. I pray that you will discover that same truth.

Notes:

1. Dave and Jan Dravecky, *When You Can't Come Back* (Grand Rapids: Zondervan, 1992), 125-126.

2. Ibid, 40-41.

3. Ibid, 106

PERSONAL QUESTIONS

1. Read Joshua 7.

   a. Why did the reconnaissance team tell Joshua that they didn't need all their troops to fight at Ai? (verses 3-4)

   b. Have you ever made a significant decision without consulting God first?

   c. What did Israel's assumption say about their attitudes? What had Israel forgotten?

d. Has your pride ever gotten in the way of asking God for help? What happened?

e. How did the Israelites respond to their defeat at Ai? (verse 5)

f. How did Joshua respond? (verses 7-9)

g. When was the last time you cried out to the Lord in despair? What was the reason? What did you say?

h. How did the Lord respond to Joshua? (verse 10)

i. How can God's response to Joshua remind you not to lose hope in the midst of failure?

j. What choices in your life may be affecting your relationship with God? Are you ready to give them up to the Lord?

k. What does verse 23 say you should do once you've identified the sin in your life?

GROUP QUESTIONS

1. Read Hebrews 12:1-13.

   a. Discuss the ways in which Achan's fall (his loss of hope) is a
      possibility for every person. (verse 1; 1 Peter 5:8; 1 John 2:16)

   b. Why is Jesus the only one who can help you maintain
      harmony with God and the hope that results from that?
      (verse 2; Hebrews 2:18; 4:15)

   c. What can happen if you take your eyes off Jesus in your fight
      against sin in the world? (verse 3b and 5-6)

d. How can you keep each other accountable in order to avoid this?

e. If God did not discipline Christians for sin, what would that prove? (verse 8)

f. Who do you respect more: those who have standards and enforce them, those who have standards but don't enforce them, or those who have no standards? Explain. (verse 9)

g. What is God's desire when He takes you through troublesome discipline? (verse 10)

h. What is the end result of chastening for those who will allow it to take its course? (verse 11) Discuss examples of how God's correction can help you grow.

i. What does verse 11 say about the discipline of the Lord?

j. How can this encourage you when we feel like losing hope?

k. Talk through the parallels between verses 12-13 and the five steps to regaining hope in this lesson:

- Take action:

- Identify the core:

- Don't rationalize:

- Deal honestly before God:

- Destroy the barrier:

1. Why is "healed" (in this context) a good synonym for restored hope? (verse 13) Share an example of a time when God "healed" you or someone you know.

DID YOU KNOW?

Confessing our sins, laying them out honestly before the Lord, would be much more direct if we acted in accordance with the meaning "confess." The Greek word is *homologeo* which comes from *homologos*, "of one mind." *Homologeo* consists of two words: *homo* meaning "same or like" and *logeo* meaning "to speak." So *homologeo* means "to speak the same," "to say the same thing as," or "to agree." Therefore, when we confess our sins, we say the same thing (agree) about our sins that God says about them. When we call sin anything else, we have not confessed because we have not agreed with God.

A Psalm of Hope

Psalm 146

In this lesson we discover why God is the God of hope.

OUTLINE

"Praise the Lord" is not a modern expression, it's a biblical one! When the psalmists of the Old Testament wrote "hallelujah" (praise the Lord), they did so for specific reasons. In Psalm 146 we find seven reasons for praising the Lord, seven ways He restores hope to the hopeless.

I. **The Argument of the Psalmist**
   A. A Strong Resolution to Hope in God
   B. A Strong Rejection to Hope in Man

II. **The Actions of God**
   A. The God of Hope Represents the Oppressed Against His Accusers
   B. The God of Hope Replenishes the Food for the Hungry
   C. The God of Hope Releases the Prisoners From Bondage
   D. The God of Hope Restores Sight to the Blind
   E. The God of Hope Raises Up Those Who Are Bowed Down
   F. The God of Hope Reaches Out to the Need of the Stranger
   G. The God of Hope Relieves the Fatherless and the Widows

If you have ever been to Chicago and taken a tour of the city, more than likely you have gone to the Bowery district and have been shown a famous landmark: the Pacific Garden Mission. The Mission provides hope, shelter, food, clothing, and a warm place for the street people of Chicago. If you listen to Christian radio, you might even have heard a program that originated with the Pacific Garden Mission called *Unshackled*. The program tells the stories of men and women whose lives have been changed through the ministry of that mission in a very "rough" part of Chicago.

More than anything else, the Pacific Garden Mission is a place where hope is offered to those who are often hopeless. Sarah Clarke and her husband, who founded the ministry, began by printing up little cards on which was printed this message:

Hope for all who enter.
Pacific Garden Mission
67 West Van Buren Street
Strangers and poor always welcome.
Special song service, 7:30 every night.

They took these little invitation cards out into the districts around the mission and distributed them to all the street people, everyone they could find. Some of the folks who got a card would go to the Pacific Garden Mission that very night, and some of them would experience the hope that comes through knowing Christ. Others would crumple the note and stick it in their pocket only to pull it out weeks or months later when they really needed help—and then go to the Mission.

In this lesson, I want to hand out such a card, so to speak, on which is written, "Hope for all who enter." You may need this card today, or you may need it sometime in the future. If you remember where this card is located in God's Word, there may be a time in the future when you will want to pull it out and read its contents. It may help to restore your hope when you most need it. My hope and my goal has always been that as you draw your attention to the Word of God, that there will be a time in your life when that particular passage will come alive again as you read it over, maybe see some things you scratched in the margin, or words that you underlined, and you will remember what God said to you on another occasion.

The card I want to give you today is Psalm 146, one of the "Hallelujah psalms." *Hallelujah* is the Hebrew word for "praise the

LORD," and Psalm 146 is the first of five psalms that begin and end with praise to God Psalms 146-150.

THE ARGUMENT OF THE PSALMIST

Psalm 146 paints a wonderful picture of hope. It is a card of invitation to those who are despairing and are desperate for renewed spiritual energy from God.

A Strong Resolution to Hope in God

The first thing you note as you begin to read the words is that there is within the psalmist's heart a strong resolution to find hope in God. In verses 2 and 3 the he writes, "Praise the LORD, O my soul! While I live I will praise the Lord; I will sing praises to my God while I have my being."

We have seen already in this study of hope that hoping in God is a decision we make, something we choose to do. The human flesh does not naturally or automatically hope in God. If we are going to have hope in Him, it will be because we, like the psalmist, choose to praise the Lord.

Twice in these two verses the psalmist says with resolution in his writing, "I will . . ." He says, "I will praise" and "I will sing" to the Lord. He reminds us that we have the opportunity to make a decision. The will is the human "chooser"—everything significant we accomplish in our lives is because we exercise our will in a certain direction. When we don't exercise our will in God's direction, it can only go in the direction of self or the world. The psalmist says he will praise the Lord as long as he lives ("while I have my being").

How often we find singing as the vehicle for praise in the psalms. (The family of "sing" words occur more than seventy times in the book.) Isaiah the prophet wrote of exchanging the "garments of praise for the spirit of heaviness" (Isaiah 61:3). We can literally sing our way out of the heaviness of despair and into the lightness of joy. Does it happen on occasion when you come to church, and before the message ever was started, before you ever opened the Scriptures to examine the Word of God, you've found your whole spirit changed through the privilege of worship and praise unto God. It is a choice that you make. The psalmist says, "I have made a resolution. I will find my hope in God!"

A Strong Rejection to Hope in Man

In verse 3, the psalmist does a little contrasting—choosing to hope in God means rejecting the temptation to hope in man: "Do not put your trust in princes, nor in a son of man, in whom there is no help. His spirit departs, he returns to his earth; in that very day his plans perish" (verses 3-4).

We live in days when our fates, humanly speaking, are in the hands of the leaders of our nation, state, and community. And every day, we discover new reasons not to place our ultimate faith in what they decide. If we were to evaluate the promises made by politicians running for office in light of how faithfully they kept those promises, it would be easy to lose hope. Too often, politicians and leaders fail—they are just as fallible as any others, and it is foolish to put our hope in them.

For those who need convincing, the psalmist gives three reasons not to trust in "princes."

Man Is Helpless; God Is Able to Help

The psalmist says that man is helpless— "Do not put your trust in princes, nor in a son of man, in whom there is no help." Man is really helpless to give you hope. But look down further in the text and notice in verse 5 that he says, "Happy is the one who has the God of Jacob for his help." There is no help in man, but there is help in God.

Man Is Mortal; God Is Eternal

Secondly, the psalmist says that man is mortal. Man is finite, limited, temporal, and terminal! The psalmist puts it this way: "His spirit departs, he returns to his earth; in that very day his plans perish" (verse 4). Even the very best of human leaders are temporal and frail. They can vanish at any moment from the stage of history with all their plans and promises unfulfilled. What real influence do leaders of the past have on the present? They die and are forgotten, replaced by others like them who will also die and be forgotten. That is not to take credit away from some leaders throughout history who have done noble things. It is only to say that all men will go into the grave.

But not so the Lord: "The LORD shall reign forever—Your God, O Zion, to all generations. Praise the LORD!" (verse 10) If you are going to put your hope in someone, put it in Someone eternal whose plan sand promises will never fail.

Man's Truth Perishes; God's Truth Is Forever

The third reason for not hoping in man is that God "keeps truth forever" and man doesn't (verse 6b). Man is a limited creature without the power or ability to always say the right thing. And when he does say the right thing, he isn't always able to follow through on what he says. Man's truth is limited, but God's truth is eternal. His word never fails.

To summarize, the psalmist is saying this about his own source for hope: "I resolve to put my hope in God, and the reasons are clear to me: Man is mortal, God is eternal. Man's truth perishes, God's truth is forever. Man is helpless, God is able to help."

THE ACTIONS OF GOD

So having decided, now, that his hope is heavenward, the last part of the psalm is some of the most encouraging truth on this subject of hope. And the question is: What can God do for those who look to Him for help? The description we are given of the kind of people Jehovah helps, makes room for all of us. The oppressed, the hungry, the prisoners, the blind, those that are bowed down, the righteous, the strangers, the fatherless and the widows. What a list! Haven't we learned so far in this study that hope springs out of hopelessness? What a list of hopeless people that is! Strangers, fatherless, widows, blind. The psalmist says, listen, there's hope for all of those folks. It kind of look like the list of guests at the Pacific Garden Mission, doesn't it?

The God of Hope Represents the Oppressed Against His Accusers

First, the God of hope stands with the oppressed against his accusers: God is the one who "executes justice for the oppressed" (verse 7). That means God is our advocate, our defender, not only against human attackers but supernatural as well. When we sin or are unfaithful to God, "We have an Advocate with the Father, Jesus Christ the righteous" (1 John 2:1). When Satan comes to attack the children of God before the throne of God (Job 1:6), Jesus Christ steps in as our Advocate and defends us against the "accuser of [the] brethren" (Revelation 12:10).

When we serve God in this world and are ridiculed and attacked by others, we can almost be on the verge of losing hope—until we remember that God comes to the aid of the oppressed.

The God of Hope Replenishes the Food for the Hungry

Secondly, the God of hope gives food to the hungry. How does God do that? In many different ways. He sent ravens to feed Elijah in one situation, then miraculously provided oil and flour in another. God could do those miracles today, and undoubtedly does in some instances. But the way God chooses to work today, primarily, is through His people, the Church of Jesus Christ.

Oftentimes, what God does is, He feeds the hungry through His own people, the Church. The New Testament says our faith is proved empty if we know of a person in need but do nothing to help meet that need (James 2:14-17). God is the one who meets that person's needs, but He does it through the generous and obedient hands of His people to whom He has given the means to help the poor and needy.

The God of Hope Releases the Prisoners From Bondage

Thirdly, God releases the prisoners from bondage. In verse 7c we find that God "gives freedom to the prisoners." He did that literally on more than one occasion: Daniel was released from the lions' den; Shadrach, Meshach, and Abed-Nego were freed from a fiery furnace; Peter, Paul and Silas were all set free from prison. God even set the millions of descendants of Jacob free from slavery in Egypt. God can physically free prisoners in multiple ways from multiple reasons when it is in accordance with His plans and purposes.

At Turning Point, we get letters almost weekly from people behind bars who will tell a story of having been incarcerated for some crime they committed and went to prison, ungodly and unsaved, and while there, through Prison Fellowship, or through a group of Christian people, were drawn into a Bible study. We get letter after letter from people who say, "We went to prison. And while we were there, we found Christ." When eternity casts its light upon those individuals, it will speak to this issue that they are better off in prison with the Lord than out of prison without Him. In prison, they were released from their bondage.

The God of Hope Restores Sight to the Blind

God is a God of miracles who can restore sight to human eyes at any time (verse 8a). As a demonstration of the power of God to validate the Word of God, Jesus performed this miracle when He was on earth. But in two cases—Saul of Tarsus (Acts 9) and the man born blind (John 9)—the gift of physical sight was accompanied by the gift of spiritual sight. Saul (who became the apostle Paul) was a persecutor of the followers of Jesus until he was stuck blind for three days. When his sight was restored, He saw Jesus as Lord. The man Jesus healed in John 9 had the same experience, characterized by his famous words, "Though I was blind, now I see."

The blindness with which Israel was afflicted was spiritual, not physical (Isaiah 6:9-10). And it was that blindness that Jesus came to remove (Luke 4:18-21). And it is that same spiritual blindness that Jesus will remove today for all who call upon His name.

The God of Hope Raises Up Those Who Are Bowed Down

God also "raises those who are bowed down" (verse 8b). Being bowed over is a classic illustration of depression—someone weighted down under the load of care and hurt, so overwhelmed with the burdens of his life that he can't even straighten up, and the God of hope comes along and straightens him out, lifts him up, and gives him hope again. When that person encounters Jesus Christ, everything about him can change. He takes Jesus' yoke upon him which is easy, Jesus' burden which is light (Matthew 11:28-30).

In our world today, it is easy to lose hope and become depressed. If you don't read the daily newspaper through the lens of God's Word, everything can look pretty terrible. Believing that man's best hope is man can lead to hopelessness in short order. Wars, the economy, disease, political scandals, personal problems—the human "frame" was not designed to carry that kind of weight. It is only when God lifts the weight off our shoulders that we are able to straighten up and stand erect.

The God of Hope Reaches Out to the Need of the Stranger

Then, the psalmist says that God "watches over the strangers" (verse 9a). Strangers in the Old Testament might have been equivalent to the homeless in our day—those who seem to be alone in the world with no one to care for them. Because the Lord watches over and protects the ravens (Luke 12:24), we know He watches over all who are created in His image. And we are His hands in this world. Too often we are hesitant to reach out to "strangers" because of fear of what might happen. We teach our children, "Don't talk to strangers"—and for good reason. And we're afraid to give money to those we don't know for fear it won't be used appropriately. We have to be cautious and sensible, yes. But we also have to continue to be God's hands and heart in this world.

The God of Hope Relieves the Fatherless and the Widows

Finally, God "relieves the fatherless and widow" (verse 9b). Watching over "orphans and widows in their trouble" is what the apostle James called "pure and undefiled religion" (James 1:27).

There are more and more single parents in our world, and wars and diseases have created orphans in unprecedented numbers around the world. God is the God who never loses track of widows and the fatherless. He knows their names and where each one is.

You may be a widow or widower, a single parent, or a child who is adopted and not sure who your real parents are. But as long as there is God, there is hope. While those situations present very real human feelings, there is a greater reality that overshadows your "aloneness": the fact that, in Christ, you are a child of the living God, the God who cares for widows and orphans. You are part of a family, the Body of Christ; and God wants that family to be His arms enveloping you with His love and support. That is the church's task—true religion—according to the apostle James.

Archbishop Desmond Tutu was a leading figure in the fight to end Apartheid in South Africa. He himself has suffered at the hands of racists in that country, and seen many of his black countrymen suffer as well. When he was asked in an interview if he was hopeful about the future of South Africa, he said, "I am always hopeful, for a Christian is a prisoner of hope . . . What could have looked more hopeless than Good Friday, but then at Easter God said from this moment on, no situation will ever again be hopeless because there is hope in God."[2]

Now, you are going to take this psalm, and you may go home and crumple it up and stick it down in your pocket and forget it's there. One of these days when you feel like a stranger, maybe one of these days when you find yourself a widow, one of these days when the world has kind of tumbled in on you, you're going to reach down into your pocket and look at that paper. Oh, yes, I remember where that place is. It's over on Psalm Street. And the address is 146. And you'll go back, and you'll read it, and God will give you hope again because He is the God of hope.

Notes:

1. https://www.pgm.org/index.php?option=com_content&view=category&layout=blog&id=14&Itemid=149

2. Thomas Giles and Timothy Jones, "A Prisoner of Hope," *Christianity Today*, 10/05/92, 39-41.

PERSONAL QUESTIONS

1. Read Isaiah 61.

   a. What situations do you feel the most hopeless in? According to verse 3, how can you rid yourself of feelings of hopelessness?

   b. According to Psalm 146:8, where is God when you are bowed down? How can this encourage you to be hopeful?

   c. What does that tell you of the importance of praise to God? How often do you take time out of your day to praise the Lord?

d. Below, make a list of reasons to praise the Lord today:

2. Read Psalm 1.

   a. Compare the phrase "trees of righteousness" from Isaiah 61 with Psalm 1.

   b. How hopeful does the man in Psalm 1 appear? From where does he draw his delight? From where do you draw your delight?

c. What is the main source of his meditation (verse 2)? How does this compare to your life?

d. What kind of tree is he? (verse 3) How can you be a "tree of righteousness"?

e. What types of fruit do you want to bear for the Kingdom of Heaven? How can you do that? How does this idea parallel with the fruit of the Spirit?

1. Read Psalm 146.

   a. Psalm 146 is considered a "Hallelujah psalm." According to the chapter, what does "Hallelujah" mean? Share ideas on how can you ingrain the idea of "Hallelujah" into every aspect of your life.

   b. How long does the psalmist say he will praise the Lord? (verse 2) Discuss why he decided to reach this point of dedication.

c. In verse 2, what is the importance of the word "will"? Talk about the importance of your choice when it comes to worshiping God. If your will doesn't go in the direction of the Lord, where will it go?

d. What do verses 3-4 warn Christians not to do? How easy is it to do this? Share examples of when you put your hope in man and it failed.

e. Who should you put your trust in instead? (verse 5) Why? (verses 3-6, 10) Is this easy to do? Why or why not?

f. Who does verse 9 say God looks out for? How does this idea relate to James 2:14-17? What does that say about how Christians should act? Give examples of how to bring this proclamation to life with the people in your study group.

g. How does John 13:35 challenge a passive Christian? What are some examples of how a Christian may fall into a passive lifestyle? Do you think this is a problem in America? How can it be fixed?

DID YOU KNOW?

The Pacific Garden Mission began as a mission Sunday school started by Sarah Dunn in Chicago. She married George Clarke in 1873, and together they opened a storefront mission that seated forty. There was a potbellied stove and Bible verses on the wall. They moved in 1880 to the building that housed the notorious Pacific Beer Garden. It was Dwight L. Moody, upon returning from evangelistic meetings in England, who suggested to the Clarkes that they drop the word "beer" and add the word "mission," resulting in Pacific Garden Mission.

HOPE FOR OUR NATION

2 Kings 22 and 23

In this lesson we discover what it takes for a nation to regain spiritual hope.

OUTLINE

What does it take for a nation to be proud of who it is and looked up to by others? A strong economy? A large military? A leader in technology? While those strengths and others have their place, in the long run, a nation maintains its hope only by keeping God at its center.

I.   **Return to the Word of God**

II. **Return to the Worship of God**

III. **Return to Prayer to God**

OVERVIEW

I n the modern era, perhaps it started in 1972 with the Watergate scandal during the Nixon presidency. What I'm referring to is the public perception that cheating and dishonesty are a commonplace at all levels of society. Once it became common knowledge that dishonesty had invaded the Oval Office of the White House, it seems that hope and optimism wavered.

To be sure, President Nixon wasn't the first American president to do something dishonest or inappropriate. But he was unfortunate enough to be the first to get caught and endure the glare of public scrutiny. Since Watergate, the suffix "gate" gets applied to any high-level scandal in Washington—and there has been no shortage of them since Watergate. So many, in fact, that scandal and dishonesty are no longer surprises. The national morality now seems to include room for a certain amount of immorality that no longer shocks the public.

Cheating has become a way of life. It seems that dishonesty has infected all areas of our society. Campus surveys tell us that one third of the college students say they would cheat every time if they were sure they would not get caught. Forty-five percent of these students said they were sure that there was no reason to lead a moral life in order to be happy or successful. Dishonesty is now presumed to be par for the course among politicians. No one takes what politicians say seriously or expects them to keep their promises. Even doctors, greedy for Medicare fees, are annually performing thousands of unnecessary operations, inflicting needless pain on helpless and trusting patients, all for the purpose of making more money.

Almost daily we read or hear of unspeakable crimes and acts committed against innocent people. And the most shocking part of it is how many of these crimes are committed by young people against women, the elderly, and even the physically challenged, sometimes for money and sometimes just for the "thrill." It seems unthinkable that in the midst of natural disasters like Hurricane Katrina, police and National Guardsmen had to be called in to keep people from looting homes and businesses.

Boston College Professor William Kilpatrick wrote a book entitled *Why Johnny Can't Tell Right from Wrong*. In the book he asks these questions: Why is it that large numbers of our young people seem to have lost their moral compass? How is it that what was clearly and unambiguously understood as being moral and appropriate forty years ago is laughable and even absurd in the minds of young people today? Why do 135,000 high school students carry weapons to school every day? Why do 25 percent of public high school students avoid using the school restrooms because they are terrified of being attacked after going inside? Why have 33 percent of high school teachers in our country become so disillusioned by the brazenly immoral behavior of students that they are considering leaving their profession? Why are suicides among young people up 300 percent in the last thirty years? Why is it that forty percent of today's fourteen-year-old girls will be pregnant by the time they are nineteen? Why?[1]

The answer, of course, is that something has gone wrong in our nation. These are not just new versions of old immorality. We have come to a place in America where the moral culture in which we are trying to raise our families is so corrupt and perverted that it is very difficult to comprehend how we can succeed. There is no answer apart from the intervention of a powerful God in the life of the nation.

But this is not the first time there has been wickedness in a nation. Wickedness has reigned throughout human history, even at the highest levels of government. In Judah, King Manasseh had been on the throne for fifty-five years. He is regarded as probably the worst king who ever served in Judah, but he was followed to the throne by his son, Amon. And the Scripture says that Amon surpassed his father in evil. In fact, he was so wicked that he was killed by his own slave after reigning only two years.

But Amon had a son by the name of Josiah, and Josiah is one of my heroes because he came to the throne of Judah in one of the darkest house of her history, and because he allowed God to work in his life. He was responsible, from the human perspective, for the greatest reversal in in the decadence of the nation that we know of in history. Interestingly enough, he became the king of Judah when he was only eight years old. He served for thirty-one years, from age eight until age thirty-nine, and we are told that his reign of righteousness began in the most unpretentious way.

When he became king, Josiah noticed that Solomon's temple had fallen into a terrible state of disrepair during the fifty-seven years of Manasseh's and Amon's reigns. So he put together a crew of craftsmen and builders to begin restoring the temple to its rightful glorious state. While these men were doing their work, cleaning out various areas of the temple complex, they found a book. Let's follow the text of 2 Kings 22:8-11:

> Then Hilkiah the high priest said to Shaphan the scribe, "I have found the Book of the Law in the house of the LORD." And Hilkiah gave the book to Shaphan, and he read it. So Shaphan the scribe went to the king, bringing the king word, saying, "Your servants have gathered the money that was found in the house, and have delivered it into the hand of those who do the work, who oversee the house of the LORD." Then Shaphan the scribe showed the king, saying, "Hilkiah the priest has given me a book." And Shaphan read it before the king.
>
> Now it happened, when the king heard the words of the Book of the Law, that he tore his clothes.

Tearing one's clothes was a way of expressing great pain and remorse. Here was Judah, God's people. They had had fifty-five years of Manasseh, and a few days of Amon, and they were so degraded and immoral in their national life that nobody even had a copy of the Book of the Law. It would be the equivalent of this country not having any Bibles anywhere. And one day they are digging around in the ruins and they find this book. They brought it to King Josiah. He read it. And God began a revival in Judah through having found the Book of the Law in the ruins of the temple. What a story!

The Bible tells us here that Josiah began to bring the Word of God back to the place of national prominence among his people. In 2 Kings 23:3 it shows how he made an issue out of this. It says here, "Then the king stood by a pillar and made a covenant before the Lord, to follow the Lord and to keep His commandments and His testimonies and His statutes, with all his heart and all his soul, to perform the words of this covenant that were written in this book. And all the people took a stand for the covenant."

Can you imagine such a moment? The King, taking the Word of God, standing up by the pillar in the central place, and reading the Word of God, and saying, "I will follow this with all of my heart and with all of my soul, and will you follow me?" And the people took a stand for God's Word.

Let's look at three things Israel did that gave renewed hope to the nation—and that would give renewed hope to our nation if we would do the same.

RETURN TO THE WORD OF GOD

The foundational act by which a nation can renew its hope for success and the blessing of God is to reestablish the Word of God as its moral and spiritual compass. This world operates today on the basis that there are no transcendent, absolute values. Our nation has embraced a new morality, an amorality, which says nothing is right or wrong. All we have to do is look around in our society to see the fruits of such a moral system. Several generations of young people have been raised with the absence of biblical influence in public schools, and it shows. We are witnessing the proliferation of behavior and actions by people in our culture that would have been considered unthinkable and unconscionable a hundred years ago. When you take God's moral code, found in Scripture, out of the public square, in time people will run wild since there is no longer a corporate conscience that separates right from wrong.

The re-establishment of the Word of God has to begin in our churches. Because God's Word has not only been lost in the moral fiber of this nation. God's Word has been put on the side burner in many churches and has absolutely no place in the life and ministry of the church. The fact of the matter is, whether the secular humanists like it or not, God has said some things are right and some things are wrong. The Ten Commandments are not the Ten Suggestions. God has said, "Thou shalt," and, "Thou shalt not."

When the church does not say what God says, the only thing it can say is what the culture says. Our nation, indeed the world, has suffered the consequences of not obeying God. Think what a difference moral purity would make (obeying God's standard of sexual abstinence outside marriage) to the spread of sexually transmitted diseases like HIV/AIDS. It doesn't matter what the area of life is—when we disobey God's standards, there will, either immediately or in the future, be drastic personal and national consequences.

The Harvest Law of Galatians 6:7 would, if embraced by our nation, result in drastic changes. If we asked ourselves what kind of harvest we would like (what kind of nation we want to be), then we would know what kinds of seeds to sow. Unfortunately, the seeds our nation has sown have resulted in a moral climate that very few people want. And if the government is unwilling to lift up the Word of God as the standard to go by, the church must do it.

RETURN TO THE WORSHIP OF GOD

Re-establishing the Word of God at the center of Israel's national life was Josiah's first commitment. But his second step came when he realized that the nation had stopped worshiping God as the Word of God commanded. The absence of Scripture led to the absence of carrying out all that Scripture requires. And in Israel— a theocracy—that means "state-sponsored" worship at the national level down to the personal level.

The central event of worship in Israel was Passover, the celebration of God's "passing over" the firstborn of the Hebrew slaves in Egypt while the firstborn in Egypt were taken. But Israel had stopped celebrating Passover. That meant they had stopped rehearsing, for themselves and their children, the greatest act of redemption the world had ever known up to that time. They had lost their gratitude for what God had done for them in rescuing them from Egypt.

When Josiah read God's instructions in the Book of the Law concerning Passover, he reinstituted the celebration and brought the people together to worship Jehovah. Second Kings 23:22 says, "Such a Passover surely had never been held since the days of the judges who judged Israel, nor in all the days of the kings of Israel and the kings of Judah." It must have been quite a celebration! But the nation was long overdue in acknowledging God's miraculous redemption of their forefathers from slavery in Egypt.

RETURN TO PRAYER TO GOD

In the parallel passage to 2 Kings 22-23, found in 2 Chronicles, we learn that in Josiah's eighth year as King, he began to seek after God. In the twelfth year of his rule, the moral reformation began— Josiah cleansed the nation of its idolatry and pagan practices. Therefore, it took four years of seeking God with all of his heart before the nation began to be cleansed of its moral ills.

As I read the history of the Church through the ages, beginning with Scripture, I find that every great revival has started with one person who was committed to seeking God through prayer. Revival always begins with prayer. What would you expect to be true of a nation that has made prayer illegal in its schools and halls of government—except on rare formal occasions? How much revival might we expect of a nation that does not pray?

There was an article in my community's newspaper concerning prayer. The headline reads, "Should Post-game Prayers Be ruled Out of Bounds?" The article told the story of three football players on the team from a local Christian high school. They began the practice of inviting players from the opposing teams to meet in the end zone after the game for a moment of prayer. The purpose was simply to acknowledge God, give Him thanks for a safe and good game, and thank Him for the privilege of healthy competition fulfilled in a sportsmanlike manner.

The newspaper had a picture of the players gathered in the end zone for prayer after a recent game. And the community became unglued. Prayer? Involving high school students from public high schools? The ACLU had already gotten involved to determine whether church/state lines were being crossed and civil rights were being violated. All because some kids wanted to give thanks to God after a football game.[2]

What in the world has happened to this country if we can't pray together voluntarily and not be written up in the newspaper as some sort of subversive group? America will only turn around as a nation when God's people begin to take prayer seriously and be as courageous as those football players were. Josiah was that kind of man, willing to stand up for what he believed and call his nation back to the Word of God, the worship of God, and be a witness for God through prayer and action.

Our personal and national hope is in God, and God alone. And God's "hope" is in His body, the Church of Jesus Christ. In the Old Testament, God told His people, "If My people who are called by My name will humble themselves, and pray and seek My face, and turn from their wicked ways, then I will hear from heaven, and will forgive their sin and heal their land" (2 Chronicles 7:14). Does that promise apply to the Church as well as to Israel? We don't live in a theocracy in America where God is the king, but we are called to be God's "salt and light" wherever we live (Matthew 5:13-16). The future of our country, the hope of our country, is wrapped up in the lives of men and women who believe in the transcendent value of God's Word, and who are not ashamed to come to church and lift up their voices in praise to God. And we are continually called to repent of our sin and seek the Lord for His forgiveness, grace and mercy (Hebrews 4:16; 1 John 1:9).

As the Church of Jesus Christ turns from her own sins and begins to pray, lives of holiness and purity will result. And those lives of holiness and purity will have a preserving (salt) and illuminating (light, revealing sin) effect on the nation as a whole. When the church begins to care more about what God thinks than what the world thinks, change will happen. When we begin to honor the Word of God in our homes, churches, places of business, and personal lives, the result will be a return to worship and prayer. And when God is worshiped and His throne begins to receive the prayers of His people, He will begin to move to restore His presence to a land where He has been pushed to the periphery for too long.

I hope you will ask yourself about the Word, worship, and prayer in your life and your family's life. What role does the world of God play? How often do you pray? Are your children learning to pray? Do you reserve worship only for church on Sunday morning, or do you worship God in your home? When Christians and their families take on the responsibility to bring God back into their lives the way Josiah brought Him back into the life of the nation of Israel, things will change. If we pray and ask God for revival, God will answer. Revival will come. But if we don't pray and ask, it won't. The principle of James 4:2 remains true: "Yet you do not have because you do not ask."

You may be thinking, "But I am just one person, just one Christian, and I am not in a place of influence in the nation or my community." That is exactly the kind of thought that will keep change from coming. As I've read history, all of the great movements back toward God have started with one such person. I'm sure there was a moment in Josiah's life as an eight-year-old king as he began to mature in his faith when he wondered, "How in the world am I ever going to turn this nation back to God?" But he did what he knew to do and God honored him. Those three young high school football players started a prayer movement by stepping out in faith. And God promises that He will meet wherever two or three are gathered in His name (Matthew 18:20).

So the issue is not who is going to do it. The issue is what are you going to do? What is your place? What role do you occupy, in your church, in your community, in this nation? There is hope for our country. Our hope is God. If you are one person filled with the Spirit and committed to doing the will of God, you can begin a spiritual revolution on your own. All it takes is one person who will hope in God.

Notes:

1. William Kilpatrick, *Why Johnny Can't Tell Right from Wrong* (New York: Simon & Schuster, 1992), 13-14.

2. *San Diego Union-Tribune*, October 31, 1992.

1. Read 1 Timothy 2:1-4.

   a. What is Paul's instruction regarding kings and those in authority? (verses 1-2a) Why is this important? (verse 2b) Do you try to pray for those in authority in your country?

   b. According to verse 4, what does God want? How does this parallel with The Great Commission? What steps can you take to fulfill God's will for your nation?

2. Read Matthew 5:13-16.

   a. Explain the metaphor Jesus uses in verse 13. How does it apply
      to the Christian's role in society? How can you be the salt to
      those who surround you at: work, school, etc.? Is there any
      part of your life you should change to be more Christlike?

   b. Why does God put light in Christians? What are you to
      illuminate? Have you ever been afraid to shine God's light
      because you're afraid of what your peers might think?

   c. What is the world supposed to see in us? And to what end?
      (verse 16) How can the world see God's light shine through you?

3. Read Matthew 5:13-16.

   a. Explain the metaphor Jesus uses in verse 13. How does it apply to the Christian's role in society?

   b. If society loses it moral "flavor," whose fault is it?

   c. Why does God put light in Christians? List some practical ways you can demonstrate God's light and love to others.

1. Read 2 Kings 22.

   a. What condition was the nation of Judah in? (verse 13b)
      Discuss how this could compare to America today.

   b. How did King Josiah react when he heard the words of the
      Book of the Law? (verse 11) How do you think he would act
      now, if he were the ruler of your nation?

   c. How did the Lord respond to King Josiah? (verse 19-20) Do
      you think the same could be true today, if the rulers of the
      world turned to God?

d. What was the first step King Josiah took in bringing the Word of God back to a place of national prominence? (2 Kings 23:3) Discuss ways that you can bring the Word of God back to a place of personal prominence in your lives. How should you respond when you have veered from God's path?

e. How can America learn from the example of King Josiah? How can the nation turn back to God? (2 Chronicles 7:14). What steps should Christians take to make this transformation possible?

2. What does this chapter tell us about revival? When is revival possible?

a. When does revival start? Discuss how you can participate in active waiting for revival.

b. Where does God promise He will meet His followers? (Matthew 18:20) How can this bring hope, when a small group feels weak against the troubles of the world?

c. How should the Harvest Law of Galatians 6:7 serve as a warning to any nation? Discuss how this can serve as a warning to passive Christians as well?

3. Read Matthew 5:13-16.

a. Explain the metaphor Jesus uses in verse 13. How does it apply to the Christian's role in society?

b. If society loses it moral "flavor," whose fault is it?

c. Why does God put light in Christians? What are we to illuminate?

d. What is the world supposed to see in us? And to what end? In your group, discuss ways that you can be a light to those in your community, your workplace, and your nation. (verse 16)

DID YOU KNOW?

The "book" discovered by the workmen during Josiah's temple renovations was a copy of the books of Moses (2 Chronicles 34:14), the first five books of the Old Testament. In 2 Kings 22:11, it is referred to as "the Book of the Law," and in 2 Kings 23:2 it is called "the Book of the Covenant." It was the covenant stipulations that Israel had failed to keep and Josiah immediately set about implementing in order to take Israel back to the first reading of the Book of the Covenant, and Israel's response: "All that the Lord had said we will do and be obedient" (Exodus 24:7).

HOPE FOR OUR CHURCH

Selected Scriptures

In this lesson we are reminded of what can restore hope to the Church of Jesus Christ.

OUTLINE

Most Christians are unaware that the number of churches relative to the American population, and the number of Americans who attend church weekly, is declining. But the church can reverse those numbers by restoring its own hope in its divine mission: to bring hope to a hurting world.

    I.   **There Is Hope for Our Church If We Do Not Forget Our Motive**

   II.   **There Is Hope for Our Church If We Do Not Forget Our Mandate**

 III.   **There Is Hope for Our Church If We Do Not Forget Our Method**

 IV.   **There Is Hope for Our Church If We Do Not Forget Our Ministry**

Statistics vary, but there are somewhere between 350,000 and 375,000 churches in America today. And approximately 40 to 45 percent of Americans profess to attending a church or synagogue on a weekly basis. While that seems like a lot of churches and a lot of people attending them, the picture is not a very positive one.

In 1963, 65 percent of the American people said they believed in the absolute truth of all the words in the Bible. Within fifteen years, by 1978, that number had declined to 38 percent. And by the early 1990s only 32 percent of the American people believed that the words of the Bible are true. And the number of churches relative to the population of Americans has been decreasing as well.[1]

We are living, as the late theologian Francis Schaeffer once said, in a post-Christian world.[2] He meant we no longer can depend on a majority of the American people having an understanding of Christian truth and biblical content. The time was when America was considered a Christian country, but that is no longer true. There is a story that might help you understand how drastically this has affected all of us:

> During World War II, after Hitler blitzkrieged his way across France, demanding the unconditional surrender of the Allied Forces in the European theater, thousands of British and French troops dug in along the coast of Northern France in a last ditch effort to hold off the German forces. Trapped on the beaches of Dunkirk, they knew they would soon be obliterated by the Nazis. But "during that agonizing period, it is said that the British soldiers broadcast a terse message across the English Channel, just three words. The words were, 'And if not . . . .' Was it a code? No." It was a reference to the Old Testament episode when Shadrach, Meshach and Abednego stood before King Nebuchadnezzar and his fiery furnace, and they said, "Our God is able to save us, and He will save us. And if not, we will remain faithful to Him anyway." And the Brits, when they heard those words, understood them completely. They knew the biblical context. They knew what it meant. It was a code word of courage that helped them to stand strong when everything was against them.[3]

If that same message were broadcast to America today, it would be greeted by blank stares by most of the population. There is no longer a consensus of biblical knowledge among the population (or in most of the Western countries of the world).

Instead of the church being biblically conscious, today it has become market conscious. There is a greater focus on being consumer oriented rather than biblically oriented, an emphasis on doing whatever we have to do to be relevant and approved by the culture. Someone has said the church today has a "McChurch Mentality" like McDonald's. We go to McDonald's for a Big Mac. Tomorrow it's Wendy's salad bar, or it's the wonderful chicken sandwiches at Chick-fil-A, and the church has become just another retail outlet, just a place where people change congregations, and preachers, and even denominations—just the way they change banks and groceries. If this doesn't meet my need, if this doesn't fulfill me, then I'm going to find someplace that will.

The hope for the Church of Jesus Christ in America, and the world, is never to lose sight of her purpose. No church sets out to compromise its integrity and move away from its purpose, but it does happen. And it happens when churches fail to continually affirm their purpose through the teaching and preaching of the Word of God. If Scripture does not remain the bedrock of the church's life, the mission will soon be watered down by pressure from the world.

In this lesson we'll look at four things the church must do in order to maintain any hope for fulfilling her Christ-ordained mission.

THERE IS HOPE FOR OUR CHURCH IF WE DO NOT FORGET OUR MOTIVE

There is hope for our church if we do not forget our motive. The church's motive is to exalt the Lord God. The church's motive is expressed well in the verse I chose as my life verse when I was a young man, Colossians 3:23: "And whatever you do, do it heartily, as to the Lord and not to men." Everything we do in our personal lives and in the church is to be done for the Lord, not for our own gain. Whatever God gives us to do in our vocational life, as well as in our family and personal life, should be done with excellence— in a way that honors Jesus Christ.

In our churches, if we have nice buildings and great choirs and orchestras and other programs, it is not so we can be praised or applauded. The applause goes to God who makes all things possible for whom all things are undertaken and accomplished. There's a fine line that separates the Spirit from the flesh, in the Christian life. Churches can do all sorts of noble things for Christ—evangelism, missions, discipleship, ministry to the poor. But if we are not careful, we can allow carnal motives to take over. We can do great things for Christ in order to make ourselves look good. God will not support those who aspire to greatness for carnal reasons (James 4:6).

An example of not doing our best for God is found in the Old Testament book of Malachi. When the exiles returned to rebuild Jerusalem and the temple, the sacrifices were reinstated. However, many Israelites were bringing God their worst instead of their best. Instead of bringing the best of their flocks to sacrifice before God, they brought the poorest animals they had (Malachi 1:6-14). And we've been doing that in our churches for years, haven't we? We've been giving God the leftover of our time, the leftover of our money, the leftover of our energy and abilities. If there is any hope for our churches, then we need to understand what our motive is in all that we do.

The Word of God says, "By this is my Father glorified, that you bear much fruit" John 15:8. First Corinthians 6:20 says, "For you were bought at a price. Therefore, glorify God in your body and your spirit which are God's." Our primary motive must be to honor Christ in all things—to serve Him heartily in everything we do.

THERE IS HOPE FOR OUR CHURCH IF WE DO NOT FORGET OUR MANDATE

What is the mandate of the Church? The Great Commission given by Christ to His disciples was to evangelize the world and make disciples in all nations (Matthew 28:19-20). We do not exist for ourselves—we exist as servants of Jesus Christ (Romans 1:1) to carry out His command.

There is hope for every church that makes the mission of Christ its own mandate—its reason for being. I grew up in an era when knocking on doors, telephone evangelism, and crusade evangelism were the norm. Those are almost all gone. There are fewer full-time preaching evangelists today since they have fewer places to go. How are we going to penetrate a culture that does not accept Jesus Christ, that rejects the Biblical mandate? Times have changed but the mandate has not. It is still the church's mission to take the Gospel into all the world and make disciples of the nations.

Our culture today is filled with men and women who wake up one day and realize they are in their forties. The idea of knowing God rarely crosses their mind. Survival is the main thing they are concerned about on a daily basis. The have a couple of teenage kids whom they don't understand. They have a job they're not particularly crazy about. And they have a large mortgage payment that keeps them tied to that job. They suddenly realize they are not sure who they are, why they are here, or where they are going. Their life has no compass, no central theme around which it is organized. And they have little hope of anything getting much better or being any different.

"Hopeless" is a good word to describe these individuals. Instead of hope, they focus on momentary bits of pleasure here and there—illicit pleasure, if need be. Just something to break up the boredom and medicate the angst they feel about their life. They welcome the end of the day so they can go to sleep, but they dread the alarm clock in the morning because it means they have to go back to that which they don't like.

Ephesians 2:12 describes these people, of whom our culture is full: "Without Christ . . . having not hope and without God in the world." The forty-year-old man who approaches midlife without purpose and identity and hope is that person (as an example) to whom the Church of Jesus Christ has been sent. The world is filled with people who are turning to everything the world has to offer to find meaning and hope: success, money, drugs, alcohol, sex, power, and prestige. They are trying to fill the void that hope, through Jesus Christ, is supposed to fill.

These people, for the most part, are not going to be reached through open-air crusades in stadiums. Nor are they going to allow some "religious" strangers to come into their home and tell them about Jesus. But they will do one thing: They will respond to genuine relationships and friendships. More than anything else in their life, that is what they are looking for—human contact. If the church will continue to do what it has made significant progress with in recent decades—friendship, or relational evangelism—it can bring hope to people who are hungry to find it. Their lives are often filled with offensive beliefs and practices, but so were ours when Jesus called us. So we have to love them the same way Jesus loved us.

The mandate of the Church is to take the Gospel of the love of Christ into the world. And the best way we can do that is by allowing Christ to touch people as establish relationships with them. That is the world to which God has called us. And the only way there is any hope for this church is if we remember what our mandate is, to reach a lost and dying world.

THERE IS HOPE FOR OUR CHURCH IF WE DO NOT FORGET OUR METHOD

The third lifesaver of hope for the church is not forgetting our method. Unfortunately, today the Church of Jesus Christ is trying all kinds of worldly methods to accomplish her mandate, but there is only one method Scripture sets forth: the edification of believers.

For a long time, the church has labored under the misconception and misinterpretation that pastors were the ones responsible for carrying out the mandate of the church: winning people to Christ and discipling them in the faith. But that is completely impossible for one person to do. Ephesians 4 is the passage of the New Testament that makes clear how the church is to accomplish her mission: The way the church is supposed to function is, when it comes together it is trained, and taught, and built up, and strengthened, and then we are set loose as the church to go out and make a difference in the world. To encourage and edify and grow up the Church of Jesus Christ.

And how are the members of the church built up and edified? Certainly by the spiritual gifts God has given them, but also through the consistent teaching for the Word of God. Psalm 119:130 says, "The entrance of Your words gives light; it gives understanding to the simple." More than any other single thing, the Word of God is what will thoroughly equip the believer for "every good work" (2 Timothy 3:16-17). It is what is "living and powerful, and sharper than any two-edged sword . . . and is a discerner of the thoughts and intents of the heart" (Hebrews 4:12). The Spirit uses the Word of God in the believer's life to transform his mind (Romans 12:2) and ultimately his character. And it is that transformed character that goes out into the world, through which Jesus Christ reveals Himself (Galatians 2:20).

The goal of the Christian life is to be transformed into the image of the living Word of God, Jesus Christ (Romans 8:29). That happens when the written Word of God becomes embedded in our heart, takes root, and springs up and bears the fruit of the Spirit (Galatians 5:22-23). We become like Christ as the Spirit causes us to yield to His transforming work in us so that Jesus Christ might continue to do His work in the world.

Only through a regular diet of the written Word of God—through personal study and public preaching—will we be transformed into the image of the living Word. That is the method God has ordained for the church to accomplish her mandate in the world.

THERE IS HOPE FOR OUR CHURCH IF WE DO NOT FORGET OUR MINISTRY

Finally, there is hope for our church if we do not forget our ministry. Our motive is to exalt the Lord God. Our mandate is to evangelize the world. Our method is to edify believers, to grow them up in Christ. Our ministry is servanthood. If we try to hit people over the head with the Bible instead of loving them with love of Christ, we will have failed in our ministry. God has called us to minister to a hurting world. As the old saying goes, "Nobody cares how much you know until they know how much you care." The church must make a priority of asking God to show us where people are hurting, regardless of where they are (or aren't) in a relationship with Christ, and serve them in whatever way we can.

We need to understand that you can preach the Word of God all you want, but if people don't know that you care about the hurts they have, they won't even hear what you are saying. Many churches today are using their facilities and resources to minister to various segments of their communities. The goal is not to preach the Gospel to people who are hurting, but simply to serve them and encourage them in whatever way we can. The Gospel of Christ's love gets preached nonverbally through these ministries in ways that may be even more effective than a verbal presentation. Often people come to Christ through support groups started and opened up to individuals in the community. I know people who have become Christians as a result of attending a support group in our church.

God has given us compassion. Our church was perhaps like many in that we were unaware of how many people in our own community were filled with despair and hopelessness. When we began to reach out to them, we found them more than willing to receive our offers of service. God uses the ability that we have to minister to other people to give us a hearing for the Gospel. It is not unusual for churches, when they reach a certain size, to become so consumed with their own maintenance that they lose sight of the ministry opportunities all around them. They have mission programs that impact the four corners of the globe but fail to see the hurting on their own doorstep.

On New Year's Day, 1929, Georgia Tech University played UCLA in the Rose Bowl in Pasadena, California. During that game a UCLA player named Roy Riegels recovered a Georgia Tech fumble, got turned around, and started running toward the wrong goal line. He ran nearly sixty-five yards in the wrong direction before Benny Lom, one of his own teammates, caught up with him and tackled him just before he was about to score a touchdown for Georgia Teach. When halftime came, everyone wondered what the UCLA coach would say to Riegels and whether he would get to play in the second half.

While all the rest of the UCLA players gathered in the locker room for the halftime review, Roy Riegels sat down in a corner with a towel over his head and cried like a baby. The UCLA coach said very little to the team during halftime, but when the time-keeper announced there were only three minutes left in the halftime break, he made his announcement: "The same team that played the first half will start the second half."

The players began to file out of the locker room onto the field— all except Roy Riegels. The coach went over to where he was sitting and said, "Roy, didn't you hear me? The same team that played the first half will start the second half."

"Coach," the weeping player said, "I can't do it to save my life. I've ruined you, I've ruined the University of California, I've ruined myself. I couldn't face that crowd in the stadium to save my life."

The coach put his hand on Riegels' should and said, "Roy get up and go back in. The game's only half over." Roy Riegels joined his team, and those Georgie Tech players will tell you they have never seen a man play football like Roy Riegels played in the second half.[4]

I can't begin to count the number of times I have been like Roy Riegels. I've taken the ball and run in the wrong direction and been too embarrassed to face Him as a result. But it never fails that God has restored my hope by sending me back into the game, reminding me that the game is only half over. That is the hope the world needs to hear today. And the only way they will hear it is from the Church of Jesus Christ—those who have been forgiven and sent back into the game themselves countless times.

The church can regain her hope and be able to offer hope to the world if we remember our motive is to exalt the Lord God; our mandate is the reach this world with the Gospel of Jesus Christ; and our method is through encouraging and building up and edifying believers.

Notes:

1. *International Christian Digest*, July/August 1992.

2. Francis A. Schaeffer, *Death in the City* (Downers Grove: InterVarsity Press 1969), 27.

3. Charles Colson, *Being the Body* (Nashville: W Publishing Group, 2003), 370.

5. Haddon Robinson, "A Little Phrase for Losers," *Christianity Today*, 10/26/92, 11.

PERSONAL QUESTIONS

1. Read Matthew 22:37-40.

   a. What did Jesus say was the greatest commandment of all? (verse 37) How are you living out this commandment in your life? Do you ever struggle with this mandate?

   b. How is 1 Corinthians 10:31 a parallel to this idea? How should this affect how you live your daily life? Use examples.

   c. What did Jesus say was the second greatest commandment? (verse 39) How should this play out in your life?

d. How would you define "neighbor"? Who is your neighbor?

e. How would obedience to this command change a church's ministry? Would the church minister more to itself or to those outside the church? How would it change your ministry?

f. How does this passage of Scripture help to simplify the spiritual life? How could loving God and loving others serve as good measures for every action in your life?

2. What is the greatist attribute to be found in a servant? (1 Corinthians 4:2)

3. The mandate of the Church is found in all four Gospels in various forms. Summarize each in your own words, identifying what is unique about each:

- Matthew 28:18-20

- Mark 16:15

- Luke 24:47

- John 20:21

a. How often do you hear the "mandate" or "mission" of the Church taught or preached at your church?

b. Before studying this lesson or reading the four passages above, how would you have described the mandate (mission) of the Church?

c. What part are you personally playing in fulfilling that mandate?

d. From what you can see, why has the Church not completed her mandate after 2,000 years?

1. Discuss:

    a. The Great Commandment (Matthew 22:37)

    b. The Great Commission (Matthew 28:19-20)

    c. How are these two connected? How is fulfilling the Great Commission a reflection on how well you are obeying the Great Commandment?

    d. Share examples of ways which you can fulfill both.

2. Talk about the four advantages of a steady diet of the Word of God from 2 Timothy 3:16-17.

   a. Doctrine:

   b. Reproof:

   c. Correction:

   d. Instruction:

e. What is the goal of the Word of God in a person's life over time? (verse 17) What are some examples of "every good work"? What are the "good works" to which Paul is referring in Ephesians 2:10?

3. Explain the advantages of the Word of God according to Hebrews 4:16.

a. Living and powerful (see Isaiah 55:11)

b. Piercing between soul and spirit

c. Discerner of thoughts and intents

d. Share your method for feeding on the Word of God consistently.

4. What is the greatest attribute to be found in a servant (steward)? (1 Corinthians 4:2) Share examples of how the group can live this out.

DID YOU KNOW?

On August 6, 2007, the Barna Group released results of a survey of Christian adults related to challenges to their faith. Of eight specific challenges, the following numbers represent the percentages of the adults identifying with each challenge: having enough time to devote to their faith (34 percent); helping their children become spiritually mature (30 percent); helping their spouse become spiritually mature (23 percent); personally growing spiritually (21 percent); understanding the Bible (20 percent); finding a church home (19 percent); getting direction from God (18 percent); practicing principles of the faith (18 percent).[5]

HOPE FOR OUR FAMILIES

Selected Scriptures

In this lesson we learn three ways to restore hope to our families.

OUTLINE

Never has the family fallen on such hard times as it has in modern America. The blueprint for making the family work is still available in Scripture. All that is needed is for the Church and responsible individuals to nurture the family back to a place of health and hope.

I. Return to the Word of God as the Source of Authority

II. Re-establish the Church as the Place Where Families Are Nurtured and Encouraged

III. Resolve to Take Responsibility for Our Families

OVERVIEW

Family life today is so different from what it was 25 years ago that to try to put them together in the same picture is almost impossible. Here's a favorite passage of mine from the "eminent theologian" Erma Bombeck:

> Why did the home-cooked meal become extinct? Maybe because it deserved to die. I got to the point where I couldn't even get the family to the table at one time. When I announced, "Dinner!" the entire family swung into action like a precision drill team . . . . For no apparent reason, my husband would exit to the bathroom with two volumes on Churchill. One child would pick up the telephone and dial a random number, another would grab a basketball and go outside to shoot baskets, and one of them would take a bus somewhere.

> When Donna Reed first invented the dinner hour, it was designed to be a gathering place for the family, where they would sit around and exchange pleasantries about the asparagus. Our family, when we got together, sounded like we were attending a lynching. The problem at family dinners is that no one can agree on what is considered to be a "fit topic to discuss at dinner time." Children tend to talk about things that take away your interest in food—and living.

> At one meal alone, I heard a description of the underside of the tongue and a rumor of what popular food contains rats' nostrils . . . Men prefer to talk about money. Within minutes they can make you feel guilty for asking for seconds on the salt. They also take the opportunity to lay on the family their famous lectures on, "An 'E' on the gas gauge does not mean evacuate." "Don't reach out and touch somebody unless it's a collect call." And my all-time favorite, "Why do we have to straighten his teeth? He never smiles anyway."[1]

Erma Bombeck pretty much gave up on getting her family together at one time at the same table for enough minutes to eat a meal together. Many have given up, and modern families have become decentralized—scattered. And that's just one of the ways they've changed.

A book by Martin Seligman offers great insights into the effects of changing social structures on our society. He says that one reason disease and depression are so much more common, or at least more noticeable, is that many of the institutions that provide common support for our lives are gradually disappearing.

In a section in his book called "The Waning of the Commons," he describes three support systems we are losing. First, our faith in a transcendent God. Second, a lack of faith that our nation (government) can provide the comfort and security that it has in the past. And third, families are failing to provide support for individuals facing challenges.

In 1962 the government of our nation made a symbolic decision: to take God out of public schools. The day after that decision was made, there was likely no discernible difference. But 55 years later, the difference is all too easy to detect. Generations of children have been raised to believe, at least from the government's perspective, that God is "not there"—that He is irrelevant. All one has to do is look at public schools today—policemen walking the halls, school shootings, attacks on teachers, drugs and firearms on campus—and ask whether making God irrelevant to education was a wise decision.

But there were other events that shook our confidence in our "national" support system. On November 22, 1963, President John F. Kennedy was assassinated in Dallas, Texas, the very city where I was enrolled in seminary at that time. We'd read about Abraham Lincoln being assassinated in the context of the Civil War, but we certainly didn't think the same thing would ever happen again. It was a message that said, "Something is wrong in the family called 'America.'"

A few years past, 1968 came along, and Martin Luther King, Jr. was killed. A few months later Bobby Kennedy was killed. We went through the Watergate scandal. We watched one of our presidents, in whom we had put our trust, stand in shame before national cameras and resign from the presidency. Some may have even forgotten that during that same time the vice president had to resign due to financial improprieties.

In the decades that most of us have been alive, abortion has been legalized, and the right to print and broadcast pornography has been established by the courts. Our tax dollars have been used to pay for things that 100 years ago would have been unmentionable, much less legal. Homosexuality has come out of the closet, and along with it HIV, AIDS, and everything else that has torn away at the fabric of who we are as a nation.

In other words, we no longer live in a nation that feels like "home" to those of us who hold biblical values and try to live our lives by them. We feel like strangers (as Scripture says we are) in a foreign land as we make our way toward heaven. While that's not a surprise, biblically speaking, it is disappointing and disconcerting to see our nation move from being a Christian nation to a post-Christian nation in such a short time. The culture is not getting better in which children grow up today. And then, if that were not enough, many in our nation have decided that we don't need God anymore.

Even sadder, many churches don't seem to need God either. In so many churches that you and I are aware of, God is there as a sort of a bystander who watches over all the other things that happen. He is treated as a kindly old grandfather who pats children on the head as they come into church, not the Lord God Almighty, Creator of heaven and earth, Redeemer and Judge of all mankind. Because leaders have excused God from active participation in many churches, those who attend don't have any personal connection to Him. They can go to church week after week and never really feel or sense the presence of God among God's people.

The real thing that's happened is our families have lost their bearing. If the nation doesn't offer support and many churches don't offer support, what about the family? Abortion has had a part in that because we have devalued human life. The family as a social cornerstone has been terribly devalued and almost destroyed.

If you think about the devaluation and deterioration of the major support systems in our lives, you realize that Martin Seligman is right in what he wrote. And you realize that the three support systems put in place by God are all suffering significantly:

1. In Genesis 1-3, God established the family.

2. In Genesis 9, after the Flood, God instituted human government.

3. In Acts 2, the Church of Jesus Christ came into existence.

God started three things: the family, the government, and the Church. The enemy of your soul and mine has made a major assault on every single one of those because he knows that if those three things can be destroyed, then the Gospel will no longer have a venue in our world. He knows that if he can destroy the support structures God put in place for the human race, that people will become hopeless. Without the family, the Church, and the government, where will people turn for help? And what will happen to the Gospel? If the Church fails to be a good steward of the Gospel, and the government outlaws it, and families are too shattered to teach it to their children, what progress will the Gospel make?

In light of the changing times we live in, every Christian needs to do three things to keep hope alive in a (sometimes seemingly) hopeless world.

RETURN TO THE WORD OF GOD AS THE SOURCE OF AUTHORITY

Returning to the Word of God as the ultimate source of authority is priority number one for every Christian—especially when it comes to keeping our families together and strong. The family was God's idea. God created the family and gave us instructions in His Word for how it should function. If we are going to have successful families that serve as a source of help and a beacon of support in this world, we are going to have to maintain them God's way.

The phrase "family values" has become a catchword in our society, especially among those running for national political office. Everyone wants to be the "candidate for family values," but no one wants to define what that term means. The only place we'll find a definition of true family values is in the Word of God. Any so-called family values that are different from God's will not be sufficient to provide the kind of hope and support family members need.

In fact, even in the book of Genesis in areas where you and I would not choose to read, there is a subtle reminder to us of the importance of the family. In those passages where it says "He begot . . . and he begot . . . and after he begot he begot . . . ." is the eternal God saying to us the family is important information to write down. God cares about families.

In Exodus we find two of the Ten Commandments focused on families: Spouses not committing adultery and children honoring their father and mother. If our society did nothing more than obey those two commandments, the state of the family would be radically transformed. But so many people think God's commands take all the fun out of life. But there is nothing fun about the aftermath of adultery and rebellion.

Throughout the rest of the Old Testament, we find the good and the bad of the family. The good is in Ruth, Esther, Psalms, Proverbs, and Song of Solomon. The bad is in many of the kings of Israel, including David and Solomon, and the people of Israel themselves at the time of the restoration when divorce was rampant. Malachi told the people that when the prophet Elijah appeared in the future, the hearts of fathers and their children would need to be turned back to one another (Malachi 4:6). That prophecy does not bode well for the future of the family at the end of this age.

From Genesis to Malachi, God did not change His family values one iota. Nor did His desires for the family change in the New Testament where we have the beautiful pictures of the birth of John the Baptist and Jesus of Nazareth.

God thought so much of the family that when He wanted to send His Son to this earth, He brought Him through a family, and for 33 years Jesus Christ lived and moved in a human family just like yours and mine. Could Jesus have gone without one? Absolutely! God could have dropped Jesus Christ in the middle of this planet without any relationships at all. But He chose to put Jesus Christ here in the midst of a family to make a statement, that the family is important to God.

Read through the rest of the New Testament, and you will find over and over illustrations on the importance of the family. If you want to know how the family works, there are three passages in the New Testament you can read: Ephesians 5:22-6:4; Colossians 3:18-21; and 1 Peter 3:1-7. In those passages are all the principles any family needs to build and enjoy a family that brings joy and support to the members. If we are going to return our families to a place of hopefulness, we are going to have to return to God's Word as the source of authority. Books on marriage may or may not help. It all depends on whether you follow the Book on marriage that God has written. Only in it are the values and directives needed to build families where hope is found.

RE-ESTABLISH THE CHURCH AS THE PLACE WHERE FAMILIES ARE NURTURED AND ENCOURAGED

Once families are begun and built on the foundation of Scripture, they need to be nurtured and encouraged. And that's where the local church has a vital role to play. The church needs to be reestablished as a refuge and stronghold and defense for families in our modern societies.

If I may use a bit of a gruesome metaphor, let me suggest that when it comes to families, the church has been running an ambulance service at the bottom of Failing Families Cliff. In other words, we wait until disaster strikes, and then run in and try to pick up the pieces and put them back together again. What we should be doing is running a Healthy Family Clinic at the top of the cliff, putting guardrails in place so that our families never get near the edge of the cliff in the first place.

I'm all for restoration and healing, and I thank God for the many churches that provide excellent counseling services for those families that find themselves in difficulty. But just as preventative medicine is much more practical and less expensive than major surgery, so creating nurturing environments in church would be better than trying to put broken families together again.

So, what should churches do? We definitely need to keep the "ambulance service" running. Not every family will avail itself of the preventative measures that are available; there will be some who go over the cliff and will need rescuing. But it's important to teach, train, mentor, and nurture the families in their care so they never need the ambulance at all. Enduring marriages are marriages that are carefully entered into. In fact, the statistics today are overwhelming that the later in life young people get married, the less incidence there is of marriage default. We need to have in-depth premarital counseling—work hard to find trouble spots in relationships that might result in marital conflict and divorce down the road. Indeed, the most successful premarital counseling programs are those that assume couples shouldn't get married until they can prove that they are wise enough, mature enough, and committed enough to carry out God's plan for marriage for the rest of their lives.

Churches must get creative about nurturing and encouraging their families! We don't live in a "Father Knows Best" TV sitcom any longer. The threats against the family are much higher than before. The last fifty years have seen the tide in America turn against marriage and the family. But the bulwark of God's Word is standing as firm as ever. If churches will take God's timeless truths and communicate them in creative ways, they can become places where husbands, wives, and children can regain their hope.

RESOLVE TO TAKE RESPONSIBILITY FOR OUR FAMILIES

What will it take to return to the Scriptures and reestablish our churches as nurturing environments for families? Resolve! We have to step forward and say, "I am going to take the responsibility for my family's spiritual and emotional health and well-being."

We live in a culture where blame shifting has become an art. We blame our parents, our environment, the government, our finances, the economy, our genes, and pure chance. The idea of taking personal responsibility for past failures and future successes is not popular. It is easy to blame government, the church, or others for problems in your own family. But that doesn't work. Blaming others is not where change takes place. Anyone who wants a family filled with hope must create that kind of family himself. Let me mention briefly four New Testament families that can serve as a model for those who want to bring about changes in their own.

The first is the family of Cornelius. He was a Centurion. And he was a family man. In fact, the Bible says in Acts 10 that Cornelius was seeking after God, and he brought his family together on a regular basis, and they sought after God. They didn't know God, but they wanted to. What happened was God heard his prayer and sent Peter to talk to Cornelius, and Cornelius had the marvelous experience of knowing God personally. And you know what happened? The Bible says in Acts 10 that when Peter came to Cornelius's family, not only was Cornelius converted, but the whole household came to know Christ.

In Acts 16 we meet another Gentile named Lydia, a successful businesswoman in the city of Philippi. She was evidently wealthy as she owned a house and had servants. She was a seller of the purple fabric for which her home city, Thyatira, was famous. Some single mothers today feel disadvantaged without a husband to help bring their family together. But Lydia is possibly an example of a single mother who led her household to faith in Christ and allowed a church to be started in her home.

In the same chapter of Acts is the story of another Gentile, a Philippian, who worked at the jail where Paul and Silas had been incarcerated. When Paul and Silas were miraculously set free from prison, but did not run away, the jailer was filled with fear and asked, "Sirs, what must I do to be saved?" Paul and Silas told him, "Believe on the Lord Jesus Christ, and you will be saved, you and your household." So the jailer gathered all his family together to hear the Gospel message, and they all believed and were baptized. This is what it means to take the responsibility for your family's spiritual well-being.

Finally, in Acts 18:8 we meet a man by the name of Crispus, a Jew in charge of the synagogue in Corinth. He was a religious leader, steeped in the ways and traditions of Judaism, who had not known

Christ until hearing Paul preach about Him. He came to Christ and he brought "all his household" together and they believed and were baptized.

Here are examples of three men and one woman who were the heads of their households. They took responsibility for the spiritual health of their family and servants (household) and united them around faith in Christ. When I read these stories, it becomes clear to me we have to step up to the line and take responsibility for our families. We can't go on hiding behind our busy careers. We can't go on saying that's the woman's job. There can be no excuses for not restoring hope to the family. Scripture, the church, and initiative can make it happen.

Notes:

1. Erma Bombeck, *Family—The Ties That Bind...and Gag* (New York: Ballantine Books, 1988), 57-58.
2. Martin P. Seligman, *Learned Optimism* (New York: Alfred A. Knopf, 1991), 284.

PERSONAL QUESTIONS

1. What are some signs that show that America has turned its back on God? Are the effects of these signs pronounced?

2. Why do you think seeing God as both a God of love while also Lord Almighty Judge of all mankind is important? What happens when you only look at one side of Him? Do you ever have a tendency to only look at the side of God that you want to see?

3. Does the Word of God have a place in your daily routine? If not, how can you make Bible Study part of your life?

4. What role does the church place in the nurturing of your family? Are you modeling your faith?

5. Read Ephesians 5:22-6:4.

   a. Summarize the instruction given to wives. (Ephesians 5:22-24)

   b. What is the husband's chief responsibility? (Ephesians 5:25-30)

   c. What are Paul's instructions to Christian children? (Ephesians 6:1-3)

d. How do each of these mandates play out in your life? What were the effects of following/or not following these instructions?

e. Since Paul is writing to the Church, not Israel, why is that promise included here in Ephesians 6:3? How can this serve as an encouragement to follow God's instruction?

f. What guidance does Paul give men in their role as fathers in Ephesians 6:4?

g. How is "training" illustrated in Deuteronomy 6:6-9? How can you "train" yourself to follow the Lord's commands?

h. How is "admonition" illustrated in Proverbs 5:1-23? How can this passage instruct you on how you should live your daily life?

GROUP QUESTIONS

1. Read Exodus 20:1-17. Of the last six commandments that deal with personal relationships, three of them address familial or household matters. Discuss the reason for each command from the perspective of a nation's health.

   a. Verse 12: Honoring of parents by children. (How would this help a nation?)

   b. Verse 14: Prohibition against adultery. (How does adultery harm a nation?)

c. Verse 17: Prohibition against coveting a neighbor's property. (How would coveting affect a nation?)

d. How has the way America followed/not followed these decrees affected the way the nation is today?

2. Read Psalm 128:1-6. Describe the blessings that come to the family of the man who fears the Lord:

a. What is the condition for the blessings? (verse 1)

b. How will his work be affected? (verse 2)

c. Define what the metaphors in verse 3 are conveying about the wife and sons.

d. Talk about all the things that verse 6a implies about the stability of this family.

e. Share your ideas of how common or rare the family that is as blessed as this one is, today.

f. Name ways that your family can be strengthened through study of God's word and the local church.

g. Read Psalm 127:1-5. Discuss the key points on the family in this Psalm.

DID YOU KNOW?

I n an attempt to find out what makes 13- to 24-year-olds happy, the Associated Press and MTV teamed up to ask 100 questions to 1,280 Americans from that age range. The number one source of happiness for most of the respondents was "spending time with family." Nearly 75% of the respondents said that their relationship with their parents makes them happy. Being sexually active leads to less happiness among 13- to 17-year-olds. Close to half said that religion and spirituality are very important, and belonging to an organized religious group is also a significant source of happiness.[3]

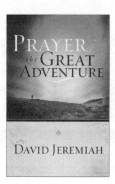

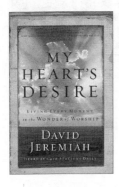

MY HEART'S DESIRE

Worship is meant to be a continuous part of life for followers of Christ. Yet, for some, worship has lost its wonder. In *My Heart's Desire,* Dr. Jeremiah shares ways in which we can experience God's presence every day through a lifestyle of worship. He invites us to discover anew the marvel of worship and what it means to have a heart filled with praise.

RESET: TEN STEPS TO SPIRITUAL RENEWAL

God gave Nehemiah two tasks: to rebuild the walls around Jerusalem and to renew the faith of the Jews. In doing so, Nehemiah shared ten steps to spiritual renewal, helping transform a faithless nation into a faithful, restored one. In this book, Dr. Jeremiah outlines these ten steps, teaching us to do as the Jewish remnant did—to reset our walk with the Lord!

For pricing information and ordering, contact us at

P.O. Box 3838
San Diego, CA 92163
(800) 947-1993
www.DavidJeremiah.org

STAY CONNECTED
TO DR. DAVID JEREMIAH

Take advantage of two great ways to let Dr. David Jeremiah give you spiritual direction every day! Both are absolutely FREE.

Turning Points Magazine and Devotional

Receive Dr. David Jeremiah's magazine, *Turning Points,* each month:

- Thematic study focus
- 48 pages of life-changing reading
- Relevant articles
- Special features
- Daily devotional readings
- Bible study resource offers
- Live event schedule
- Radio & television information

Daily Turning Point E-Devotional

Start your day off right! Find words of inspiration and spiritual motivation waiting for you on your computer every morning! Receive a daily e-devotion communication from David Jeremiah that will strengthen your walk with God and encourage you to live the authentic Christian life.

There are two easy ways to sign up for these free resources from Turning Point. Visit us online at www.DavidJeremiah.org and select "Subscribe to Daily Devotional by Email" or visit the home page and find Daily Devotional to subscribe to your monthly copy of *Turning Points*.